T0129601

An Analysis of

Kenneth Waltz's

Theory of International Politics

Riley Quinn
with
Bryan R. Gibson

Published by Macat International Ltd
24:13 Coda Centre, 189 Munster Road, London SW6 6AW.

Distributed exclusively by Routledge
2 Park Square, Milton Park, Abingdon, Oxon OX14 4RN
711 Third Avenue, New York, NY 10017, USA

Routledge is an imprint of the Taylor & Francis Group, an informa business

www.macat.com
info@macat.com

Cataloguing in Publication Data
A catalogue record for this book is available from the British Library.
Library of Congress Cataloguing-in-Publication Data is available upon request.
Cover illustration: Etienne Gilfillan

ISBN 978-1-912303-50-2 (hardback)
ISBN 978-1-912127-07-8 (paperback)
ISBN 978-1-912282-38-8 (e-book)

Notice
The information in this book is designed to orientate readers of the work under analysis,
to elucidate and contextualise its key ideas and themes, and to aid in the development
of critical thinking skills. It is not meant to be used, nor should it be used, as a
substitute for original thinking or in place of original writing or research. References and
notes are provided for informational purposes and their presence does not constitute
endorsement of the information or opinions therein. This book is presented solely for
educational purposes. It is sold on the understanding that the publisher is not engaged
to provide any scholarly advice. The publisher has made every effort to ensure that
this book is accurate and up-to-date, but makes no warranties or representations with
regard to the completeness or reliability of the information it contains. The information
and the opinions provided herein are not guaranteed or warranted to produce particular
results and may not be suitable for students of every ability. The publisher shall not be
liable for any loss, damage or disruption arising from any errors or omissions, or from
the use of this book, including, but not limited to, special, incidental, consequential or
other damages caused, or alleged to have been caused, directly or indirectly, by the
information contained within.

CONTENTS

THE MACAT LIBRARY

The Macat Library is a series of unique academic explorations of seminal works in the humanities and social sciences – books and papers that have had a significant and widely recognised impact on their disciplines. It has been created to serve as much more than just a summary of what lies between the covers of a great book. It illuminates and explores the influences on, ideas of, and impact of that book. Our goal is to offer a learning resource that encourages critical thinking and fosters a better, deeper understanding of important ideas.

Each publication is divided into three Sections: Influences, Ideas, and Impact. Each Section has four Modules. These explore every important facet of the work, and the responses to it.

This Section-Module structure makes a Macat Library book easy to use, but it has another important feature. Because each Macat book is written to the same format, it is possible (and encouraged!) to cross-reference multiple Macat books along the same lines of inquiry or research. This allows the reader to open up interesting interdisciplinary pathways.

To further aid your reading, lists of glossary terms and people mentioned are included at the end of this book (these are indicated by an asterisk [*] throughout) – as well as a list of works cited.

Macat has worked with the University of Cambridge to identify the elements of critical thinking and understand the ways in which six different skills combine to enable effective thinking.
Three allow us to fully understand a problem; three more give us the tools to solve it. Together, these six skills make up the **PACIER** model of critical thinking. They are:

ANALYSIS – understanding how an argument is built
EVALUATION – exploring the strengths and weaknesses of an argument
INTERPRETATION – understanding issues of meaning

CREATIVE THINKING – coming up with new ideas and fresh connections
PROBLEM-SOLVING – producing strong solutions
REASONING – creating strong arguments

To find out more, visit **WWW.MACAT.COM.**

CRITICAL THINKING AND *THEORY OF INTERNATIONAL POLITICS*

Primary critical thinking skill: REASONING
Secondary critical thinking skill: INTERPRETATION

Kenneth Waltz's 1979 *Theory of International Politics* is credited with bringing about a "scientific revolution" in the study of international relations – bringing the field into a new era of systematic study. The book is also a lesson in reasoning carefully and critically. Good reasoning is exemplified by arguments that move systematically, through carefully organised stages, taking into account opposing stances and ideas as they move towards a logical conclusion. *Theory of International Politics* might be a textbook example of how to go about structuring an argument in this way to produce a watertight case for a particular point of view.

Waltz's book begins by testing and critiquing earlier theories of international relations, showing their strengths and weaknesses, before moving on to argue for his own stance – what has since become known as "neorealism". His aim was "to construct a theory of international politics that remedies the defects of present theories." And this is precisely what he did; by showing the shortcomings of the prevalent theories of international relations, Waltz was then able to import insights from sociology to create a more comprehensive and realistic theory that took full account of the strengths of old schemas while also remedying their weaknesses – reasoning out a new theory in the process.

ABOUT THE AUTHOR OF THE ORIGINAL WORK

Kenneth Waltz was born in 1924 in Michigan. As a young man, he found himself personally involved in some of the major events of the twentieth century. He served in both World War II and the Korean War, before finally completing his PhD studies at Columbia University in 1954. Waltz turned his doctoral dissertation into a 1959 book, *Man, The State, and War*, which won him recognition as a leading scholar of international relations. His 1979 book *Theory of International Politics*, however, brought about a "scientific revolution" in the field, turning international relations from a branch of philosophy into a more objective social science. Waltz died at the age of 88 in 2013.

ABOUT THE AUTHORS OF THE ANALYSIS

Riley Quinn holds master's degrees in politics and international relations from both LSE and the University of Oxford.

Dr Bryan Gibson holds a PhD in International History from the London School of Economics (LSE) and was a post- doctoral research fellow at the LSE's Centre for Diplomacy and Strategy and an instructor on Middle Eastern politics in the LSE's Department of International History and the University of East Anglia's Department of Political, Social and International Studies (PSI). He is currently on the faculty of Johns Hopkins University and is the author of *Sold Out? US Foreign Policy, Iraq, the Kurds and the Cold War* (Palgrave Macmillan, 2015).

ABOUT MACAT

GREAT WORKS FOR CRITICAL THINKING

Macat is focused on making the ideas of the world's great thinkers accessible and comprehensible to everybody, everywhere, in ways that promote the development of enhanced critical thinking skills.

It works with leading academics from the world's top universities to produce new analyses that focus on the ideas and the impact of the most influential works ever written across a wide variety of academic disciplines. Each of the works that sit at the heart of its growing library is an enduring example of great thinking. But by setting them in context – and looking at the influences that shaped their authors, as well as the responses they provoked – Macat encourages readers to look at these classics and game-changers with fresh eyes. Readers learn to think, engage and challenge their ideas, rather than simply accepting them.

'Macat offers an amazing first-of-its-kind tool for interdisciplinary learning and research. Its focus on works that transformed their disciplines and its rigorous approach, drawing on the world's leading experts and educational institutions, opens up a world-class education to anyone.'

Andreas Schleicher,
Director for Education and Skills, Organisation for Economic
Co-operation and Development

'Macat is taking on some of the major challenges in university education … They have drawn together a strong team of active academics who are producing teaching materials that are novel in the breadth of their approach.'

Prof Lord Broers,
former Vice-Chancellor of the University of Cambridge

'The Macat vision is exceptionally exciting. It focuses upon new modes of learning which analyse and explain seminal texts which have profoundly influenced world thinking and so social and economic development. It promotes the kind of critical thinking which is essential for any society and economy. This is the learning of the future.'

Rt Hon Charles Clarke, former UK Secretary of State for Education

'The Macat analyses provide immediate access to the critical conversation surrounding the books that have shaped their respective discipline, which will make them an invaluable resource to all of those, students and teachers, working in the field.'

Professor William Tronzo, University of California at San Diego

WAYS IN TO THE TEXT

KEY POINTS

- Kenneth Waltz was a leading American international relations theorist of the late twentieth century. He is considered to have brought a "scientific revolution" to the study of international affairs.

- Waltz's aim in writing *Theory of International Politics* was to critique existing theories, to create a new theory to replace them, and it to test that theory with real-world international issues.

- *Theory* transformed the study of international affairs. Although the end of the Cold War* (a period of tension between the United States and the Soviet Union,* and their respective allies) in 1991 challenged its arguments, today's frictions between Russia and the United States over the crisis in Ukraine* has stimulated renewed interest in the work.

Who Was Kenneth Waltz?

Kenneth Waltz (1924–2013), the author of *Theory of International Politics* (1979), was born in Ann Arbor, Michigan, where he spent much of his childhood. After completing his primary education, Waltz attended Oberlin College in Ohio, where he first studied mathematics and then switched to economics. The outbreak of World War II,* however, interrupted his education.

After the war, Waltz returned to Oberlin to complete his Bachelor's degree, graduating in 1948. He then attended Columbia University for graduate studies, where he first majored in economics, then English literature, and finally settled on political philosophy. Waltz completed his Masters at Columbia, and then, after fighting in the 1950–53 Korean War*—in which the communist* North fought the South, with a degree of intervention and sponsorship from China, the Soviet Union, and the US—he was accepted into Columbia's doctoral program under the supervision of the international relations scholar William T. R. Fox.*

Despite having fought in two major wars, Waltz downplayed these experiences, saying they had little impact on the development of his ideas.[1]

Waltz's first major work was his doctoral dissertation *Man, The State, and War,* published as a book in 1959.[2] It would gain Waltz widespread recognition as a leading scholar in the developing field of international relations. Building on the success of that first text, Waltz published *Theory of International Politics* in 1979. It would go on to be his most influential and famous work.[3]

The importance of Waltz's *Theory* to the discipline of international relations cannot be overstated. The text brought a "scientific revolution" to the discipline and marked the start of a major theoretical debate that pitted neorealists* (who argue, very roughly, that countries have a need to compete) against neoliberals* (who argue, equally roughly, that countries have a need to cooperate). As a leading neorealist, Waltz has been described as one of the "giants" of international relations.[4]

What Does *Theory of International Politics* Say?

Kenneth Waltz's primary goal in writing *Theory of International Politics* was to answer this question: "If changes in international outcomes are linked directly to changes in actors, how can one account for similarities of outcome that persist or recur even as actors vary?"[5] In other words, Waltz wanted to know how international relations theorists can account for repeated actions among states—notably, conflicts—that have remained constant throughout history, even as states have undergone numerous and significant changes, such as political reform, revolutions, and so on.

No theoretical model had been able to account for this, Waltz believed. *Theory* was his attempt to provide one.

In the introduction to *Theory*, Waltz lays out how he intends to answer this question. First, he looks at the current theories of international politics and other approaches that claim to be important. Next, he builds a theory of international politics that seeks to remedy the defects of existing theories, which he then applies to real-world examples to show his theory's usefulness.[6]

The approach Kenneth Waltz takes in *Theory* focuses on two main ideas: 1) realism,* the school of thought that views the international system as anarchic*—that is, ungoverned by any higher authority, with states acting in the interests of their own security, and 2) the structure of the international system. The concept of realism had been around since the fifth century B.C.E., when the Greek historian Thucydides* argued in his book, *The History of the Peloponnesian War*, that politics were not rooted in matters of principle, but rather in promoting a country's own interests.[7]

Given this, modern realism is based on a number of standard beliefs:
- The international system is anarchic.
- States are the primary actors of international relations.
- States all share the goal of survival.
- States provide for their own security.

After World War II, the German political theorist Hans Morgenthau* adapted earlier realist writings into a modern theory, now known as classical realism.* That theory held that the power-hungry nature of humanity and the self-interested calculations of countries defined global politics.[8] In other words, realists believe that conflict—not cooperation—is what drives relations among states. Although Waltz shared these views, he felt that the classical realist model reduced complex matters into simple models—a process known as reductionism*—and was theoretically insufficient to answer the question that he tried to answer in *Theory.*

As a result, Waltz created a model that sought to adapt a positivist* approach to the study of international relations. He believed that a valid theory should be founded on observable evidence, and it should be possible to measure its strength by testing it against real events. That led him to conclude that certain aspects of the international system, not any particular features of the states within it, define the behavior of those states.

He went on to argue that the international system is leaderless and founded on anarchy; states are the main actors in the international system, and their capabilities and resources are distributed unevenly. This leads states to naturally compete with one another through the adoption of foreign policies aimed at advancing their own interests at the expense of others.

Why Does *Theory of International Politics* Matter?

Theory is a valuable text for students looking to understand modern international relations theory. The text marked a turning point in the study of international relations, pushing the field away from the realm of political philosophy toward the social sciences—areas that researchers can study using the scientific method of forming theories on the basis of observations and then testing those theories by observing further developments. This changed the way scholars studied the interactions between and among countries and allowed them to analyze events using a standard set of ideas.

The book, a product of the Cold War era, served as the starting point for a major theoretical debate that lasted from the 1980s to the early 1990s and led to the rise of several new schools of international relations theory:

> **neorealism***—the theory Waltz proposes in *Theory,* sometimes referred to as "structural realism"
>
> **neoliberalism***—the school of thought that cooperation between states through international institutions is likely, given the benefits of that cooperation for all
>
> **balance of threat***—a theory concerned with the ways that states decide on the extent to which other states threaten them.

This long list of theories all stemmed from the debate surrounding Waltz's text and has helped transform the way we understand the world in which we live.

The end of the Cold War posed several challenges to the neorealist school of thought, largely because the theory assumed that the competition between the United States and Soviet Union would continue. As scholars began to recognize this problem, several new schools of thought emerged. Some opposed neorealism, such as critical theory*—an approach, also referred to as the Frankfurt School, which offers a critical analysis of the assumptions on which the study of international relations is founded. The theory of constructivism,* an approach that argues that international relations are decided by the societies that make up states, also ran counter to neorealism.

Other theories attempted to adapt neorealism for the post-Cold War international scene. Among them were: 1) defensive realism,* according to which the anarchic nature of the international scene caused states to concentrate on defense to the point that conflict became likely; 2) offensive realism,* an approach emphasizing states' offensive capabilities; and 3) neoclassical realism,* a combination of neorealism and classical realism.

Although these new theories have somewhat eclipsed neorealism since the end of the Cold War, the renewal of tension between the United States and Russia in 2014 following the events in Ukraine has raised the possibility that neorealism might once again return as a leading school of thought.

In the end, *Theory of International Politics* was a revolutionary text because it changed the entire discipline of international relations. Indeed, it continues to be one of the texts that scholars in the field most often cite, with more than 12,000 citations at the time of writing, according to Google Scholar. This eclipses the number of citations of Waltz's ideological rival, the neoliberal* political theorist Robert Keohane, whose work *After Hegemony* (1984) has just over 8,000 citations.

Given its continued relevance, it is not surprising that readers continue to hail Waltz's *Theory* as one of the single most important texts in the field of international relations.

NOTES

1   Harry Kriesler, "Theory and International Politics: Conversation with Kenneth Waltz," accessed October 16, 2013, http://globetrotter.berkeley.edu/people3/Waltz/.

2   Kenneth Waltz, *Man, the State, and War: A Theoretical Analysis* (New York: Columbia University Press, 1959).

3   Kriesler, "Theory and International Politics."

4   Douglas Martin, "Kenneth Waltz, Foreign-Relations Expert, Dies at 88," *New York Times*, May 18, 2013.

5   Kenneth Waltz, *Theory of International Politics* (Reading: Addison Wesley, 1979), 65.

6   Waltz, *Theory*, 1.

7   Thucydides, *History of the Peloponnesian War*, trans. Thomas Crowley (Auckland: Floating Library, 2008), 568.

8   Hans Morgenthau, *Politics Among Nations* (New York: Knopf, 1948).

SECTION 1
INFLUENCES

THE AUTHOR AND THE HISTORICAL CONTEXT

KEY POINTS

- *Theory of International Politics* is the foundational work of neorealism,* an important school of thought in the field of international relations that emphasizes the importance of the structure of the international system.

- Waltz claimed that his experiences fighting in World War II* and the Korean War* did not affect his academic outlook.

- Waltz's approach to understanding international relations overturned the established approach. His neorealist school of thought has been successfully applied to international affairs in a world where a number of countries possess nuclear weapons.

Why Read This Text?

Kenneth Waltz's *Theory of International Politics,* published in 1979, is one of the most important texts in the field of international relations. The text revolutionized the way that scholars have studied the field by introducing an entirely new theoretical school of thought: neorealism.

When writing *Theory,* Waltz's aim was to create a theory based on the most important features of international politics: the balancing of great powers, war, and the forming of alliances. Waltz had felt that previous theoretical models such as realism* (roughly, the argument that states act in the interests of their own security) and liberalism* (roughly, the argument that states can achieve peace and mutual cooperation) had reduced complex global issues to models that were too simple—a process known as reductionism.*

> **❝** I think the most powerful shaping event occurred in August 1945 with the dropping of two atomic bombs. That was a world decisive event. The impact the bombing of Japan had on my thought about international politics was pervasive. **❞**
>
> Kenneth Waltz, "Theory Talks" interview with Peer Schouten

Like the realists before him, Waltz believed that the international system was, being ungoverned, anarchic.* He thought that states were the main actors in the international system and that their capabilities and resources were distributed unevenly, leading to competition between and among them as they sought to advance their own interests at the expense of others. Yet Waltz, with his belief that a theory should be founded on observable evidence and tested against real events, adopted a more positivist* approach to the study of international relations. He believed that the features of the international system itself, rather than any features of particular countries or their individual leaders, governed the behavior of countries within that system.

With these central points in mind, Waltz was able to provide a theoretical model that scholars could use to interpret real-world events. In doing so, his theory transformed the way scholars understood international affairs.

Author's Life

Kenneth Waltz was born in 1924, in Ann Arbor, Michigan, and attended Oberlin College in Ohio, where he studied mathematics and economics until military service in World War II* interrupted his studies. On his return, he earned a BA in economics from Oberlin.[1] Waltz continued his education at Columbia University in New York City, where he applied his economics background to the study of politics under the supervision of William T. R. Fox,* a respected realist scholar.[2]

The outbreak of the Korean War,* however, meant that his studies were once again interrupted as he fought for the US-led United Nations force against the army of communist North Korea, aided by China and the Soviet Union.* After the war, Waltz returned to Columbia to teach and complete his PhD thesis, which he later published as a book in 1959.[3] The academic community continues to hold that text, "Man, the State, and War: A Theoretical Analysis," in high regard, and it led to Waltz's rise as a major scholar of international relations.[4]

By the time Waltz published *Theory* in 1979 he was already an established academic. After leaving Columbia in 1957, Waltz taught at a number of leading colleges and universities around the US before settling at the University of California at Berkeley in 1971, where he would remain for two decades before returning to Columbia. The publication of *Theory* introduced Waltz as a leading proponent of neorealist international relations theory.

Later in life, Waltz entered into a major debate with Scott Sagan,* a scholar at Stanford University in California, who applied Waltz's theoretical model to the question of nuclear weapons. In 1997, Sagan and Waltz published *The Spread of Nuclear Weapons: A Debate*, which was updated and expanded in several later editions.[5]

Author's Background

Waltz's *Theory* was published in 1979 in the midst of the Cold War,* a time when classical realism*—which argued that it was a desire for security and stability rather than morality that guided countries' foreign policy—had become established as orthodoxy. After all, this was a time when leading international figures, such as former US president Richard Nixon* and his secretary of state, Henry Kissinger,* openly identified themselves as realists. Although we might assume that Waltz's experiences in both World War II and the Korean War had a big impact on his writing, he later claimed that these brutal conflicts did not significantly influence the development of his ideas.[6]

From the start of his career, Waltz sought to renew the study of international politics through his own "Copernican Revolution"* (a rethinking of the field as radical as that of the astronomer Copernicus's* observation in the fifteenth century that the earth revolved around the sun, and not the sun around the earth). Throughout his career, he was determined to transform the way that international relations scholars viewed events by basing analysis on scientific principles, rather than on political philosophy.

Indeed, following the publication of *Man, The State, and War* in 1959, scholars of international relations became increasingly interested in applying analytical tools—like quantitative analysis* (the analysis of numerical data such as statistics) and game theory* (the analysis of strategic choices made by participants in certain situations)—to the study of international relations. Recognizing this development, Waltz used his book to promote the application of those new types of analysis by introducing a novel theoretical model: neorealism.

NOTES

1   Harry Kriesler, "Theory and International Politics: Conversation with Kenneth Waltz," accessed October 16, 2013, http://globetrotter.berkeley.edu/people3/Waltz/.

2   Kriesler, "Theory and International Politics."

3   Kenneth Waltz, *Man, the State, and War: A Theoretical Analysis* (New York: Columbia University Press, 1959).

4   Douglas Martin, "Kenneth Waltz, Foreign-Relations Expert, Dies at 88," New York Times, May 18, 2013.

5   Scott Sagan and Kenneth Waltz, *The Spread of Nuclear Weapons: A Debate* (New York: W.W. Norton & Company, 1997).

6   Kriesler, "Theory and International Politics."

MODULE 2
ACADEMIC CONTEXT

KEY POINTS

- International relations, a specialty within the field of political science, was formally established in the late nineteenth century. Waltz wrote his book during the Cold War.*

- Liberal* theories suggest that states will cooperate whenever possible; realist* theories hold that states will tend to fight when necessary.

- Although Kenneth Waltz was inspired by earlier generations of classical realist* scholarship, he believed those classical theories were not scientific enough.

The Work in its Context

Kenneth Waltz's *Theory of International Politics* falls within the scholarly field of international relations, which is a sub-discipline of political science. Its focus is the study of the ways in which countries, empires, and non-governmental actors—international organizations such The United Nations,* corporations such as Nike or British Petroleum, or terrorist groups such as al-Qaeda* or the Islamic State of Iraq and Syria/the Levant (ISIS or ISIL)*—interact with each other.

Although scholars and philosophers have studied how groups of people or nations have interacted with each other for millennia, international relations as a scholarly discipline did not arise until the late nineteenth century. Since then, it has become a major discipline within the field of politics, with most major academic institutions offering courses to train future diplomats and policymakers. Waltz wrote the text within the context of the Cold War,* which had become an all-encompassing topic of discussion among scholars of

> **❝** The science of international politics has … come into being in response to a popular demand. It has been created to serve a purpose and has, in this respect, followed the pattern of other sciences. **❞**
>
> E. H. Carr, *The Twenty Years Crisis 1919–1939*

international relations, historians, and policymakers. That conflict for global dominance, or hegemony,* pitted the capitalist* United States against the communist* Soviet Union.*

Just as the world was dividing into two camps, so too were scholars of international relations, who split into realists* and liberals* and later into their intellectual offspring, neorealists* (who add to the realist position the argument that the structure of the international system is important to any analysis of international relations) and neoliberals* (who add to the liberal position the argument that cooperation between nations will occur, chiefly through international institutions, because of the benefits of that cooperation).

Overview of the Field

Within the field of international relations, scholarship breaks down roughly into two schools of thought: realism and liberalism. An early proponent of realist thinking was the German political theorist Hans Morgenthau.* In 1948, he published his key text *Politics Among Nations*, considered one of the leading texts in realist thought. Morgenthau argued that the flawed, power-hungry nature of humanity, rather than the calm calculations of states, defines global politics.[1] In other words, realists believe that conflict—not cooperation—is what drives relations among states.

When Kenneth Waltz published *Theory of International Politics* in 1979, it directly challenged Morgenthau's model, often referred to as classical realism.* Waltz introduced a more scientific approach to the analysis of international relations based on the assumption that state action is driven solely by a calculation of its national interests. Waltz called this new model neorealism.*

The second school of thought, liberalism, should not be confused with its traditional political definition. In the realm of international relations, liberalism bases its analysis on the idea that nations are inherently good and that political institutions should be used to promote social progress. Further, liberals believe that cooperation among countries is possible and likely, especially through international institutions like the United Nations. That is because, the argument goes, states prefer to maximize their absolute gains* rather than their relative gains* over one another. In other words, a state prefers to measure success in what that success means for itself overall, not in terms of how the balance of power is affected.

The first application of liberal international relations theory was the establishment of the League of Nations* after World War I.* This international institution was the brainchild of the American president Woodrow Wilson,* whose association with liberalism is so close that the concept is often referred to as Wilsonianism.

Around the same time as Waltz's text, however, a new paradigm emerged within liberalism. Political scientists Robert Keohane* and Joseph Nye* applied a more scientifically rigorous, economic model to the basic ideas of liberalism, known as neoliberalism.* This new model, which they put forward in their text *Power and Interdependence*, argued that states should be concerned with absolute gains rather than relative ones, because absolute gains promote cooperation among states.[2]

Academic Influences

Though the field of international relations was flush with scholarship at the time when Kenneth Waltz was writing *Theory*, the text represented a vital break with earlier scholarship. He had been inspired by a growing trend within international relations in the 1960s and

1970s, whereby theorists attempted to make their theories more scientific by incorporating quantitative techniques* (the analysis of data such as statistics), game theory* (the study of how all the participants in a certain scenario make strategic choices), and other statistical and economic tools from other, more "scientific" disciplines.

It is easy to understand why this trend would have had an impact on Waltz, who had trained as an economist and viewed classical realism as more of a philosophy than a science. He wanted to develop a scientific model that people could apply to the study of international relations.

The sociological theories of the social theorist Émile Durkheim* also influenced Waltz's concept of neorealism. Durkheim's book, *The Division of Labour in Society*, suggested that the behavior of units within systems was defined by the features of the entire system, rather than by any particular characteristic of the units.[3] Along those lines, Waltz concluded that the major causes of wars were located in the intertwined relationship of the states within an anarchical* global system, rather than in states or their leaders.

NOTES

1   Hans Morgenthau, *Politics Among Nations* (New York: Knopf, 1948).

2   Robert Keohane and Joseph Nye, *Power and Interdependence* (New York: Little, Brown, 1977).

3   Émile Durkheim, *The Division of Labour in Society*, trans. George Simpson (New York: Free Press, 1964), 257.

THE PROBLEM

KEY POINTS

- Kenneth Waltz wrote the *Theory of International Politics* during the Cold War,* when the world's two nuclear-armed superpowers where locked in a tense and dangerous competition.

- He wrote the text in response to the failure of existing theories to explain why wars had existed throughout history, even though the international world order had changed consistently over time.

- Waltz's theory of neorealism* has gone on to influence a number of scholars, among them the political scientists John Mearsheimer* and Stephen Walt,* who debated how best to understand how countries make foreign policy when faced with military and other challenges.

Core Question

Kenneth Waltz's *Theory of International Politics* is an academic attempt to understand what causes war.

When Waltz published the book in 1979, the United States was locked into a geopolitical struggle with the Soviet Union:* the Cold War.* This period in international politics was dangerous for two principal reasons: 1) global power was concentrated mainly in the hands of two superpowers,* and 2) after the two atomic bombs were dropped on Japan in 1945, the United States and the Soviet Union started competing with each other in an arms race to develop nuclear weapons. Waltz believed that nuclear weapons deeply changed everything, turning theoretical analysis on its head.

This conflict saw the direct application of realist* theory to the

> ❝ How then should we read Waltz—as one in a line of realist theorists whose work is consistent with the 'fundamental assumptions of his classical predecessors' or as a figure who has broken with the past? The answer is 'both and' rather than 'either or'. ❞
>
> Chris Brown, "Structural Realism, Classical Realism, and Human Nature"

conduct of international relations, with top American officials such as Richard Nixon,* Henry Kissinger,* and Zbigniew Brzezinski* all identifying themselves as realists. Starting in the early 1970s, the Cold War entered a period of eased tensions known as détente.*

In this context, a theoretical debate arose as a group of scholars, including Waltz and the neoliberal* thinkers Robert Keohane* and Joseph Nye,* sought to bring about a revolution in the analysis of international relations. For Waltz, the primary aim of *Theory* was to challenge the philosophical basis of the international relations theory that was widely accepted at the time and develop a new, scientific model of analysis called neorealism.*

The Participants

The field of international relations scholarship is roughly divided into two schools of thought: realism* and liberalism.*

The Greek historian Thucydides* first introduced the idea of realism in the fifth century B.C.E. in his pioneering text *The History of the Peloponnesian War.*[1] While studying the wars between Athens and Sparta, two Greek city-states, Thucydides recognized that politics was not rooted in matters of principle, but rather in the advancement of one's interests. "If [states] maintain their independence," argued Thucydides, "it is because they are strong," and the weak will, by nature, be forced to submit to their will.[2]

One of the earliest backers of modern realist thinking was the

German political scientist Hans Morgenthau.* His 1948 book, *Politics Among Nations*, is a basic text in realist theory. In it, he argued that global politics was defined by the power-hungry nature of humanity and calm calculations of countries.[3] In other words, realists believe that conflict—not cooperation—is what drives relations among states.

In contrast, within the field of international relations, liberalism is an approach based on the idea that nations are naturally good and that political institutions should be used to promote social progress. Liberals, also known as idealists, believe that cooperation among countries is possible in the absence of a hegemon*—or dominant power. They believe that cooperation often occurs in international institutions, like the United Nations or the International Monetary Fund, or in transnational non-governmental organizations, like the World Wildlife Fund. This is because states prefer to maximize their absolute gains* rather than their relative gains* over one another. In other words, countries gain more through cooperation, even though that may mean their rivals will gain, too.

Around the same time that Waltz was developing his text, a new theory emerged that built upon the liberal framework. Keohane and Nye first developed the new model, neoliberalism,* in *Power and Interdependence* (1977). This new world view was more scientifically rigorous, in comparison to previous models, having been built upon an economic model. It argued that states should be concerned with absolute gains, rather than relative ones, because absolute gains promote cooperation among states.[4]

Given the differences between neorealists and neoliberals on how to analyze international relations, it is no wonder that two separate schools of thought have developed, although neorealism—sometimes called defensive realism*—has largely dominated as the leading school.

The Contemporary Debate

Since leading scholars of international relations base their work on

Waltz's theoretical model, *Theory* stands out as the starting point for students seeking to understand the field.

Within the neorealist school of thought, key differences have emerged as other realist scholars, like the political scientists John Mearsheimer* and Stephen Walt,* have sought to build upon and modify Waltz's theoretical model. In 1983, Mearsheimer published his first book, *Conventional Deterrence*, which analyzed the use of conventional weapons—as opposed to nuclear, chemical, or biological arms—to repel military threats from neighboring states.[5] This text firmly established Mearsheimer as neorealist and dealt with key issues like nuclear weapons—a topic with which Waltz later became deeply engaged.

In 1985, Stephen Walt built upon Waltz's theoretical model in the article "Alliance Formation and the Balance of World Power," which introduced the idea of balance of threat,* setting out the criteria by which states assess threats. Two years later, Walt further developed this theory in *The Origins of Alliances*,[6] which also talked about the concept of defensive realism. This concept held that the anarchy* of the international system forced states to become obsessed with security, which ironically led to security dilemmas whereby a state's drive for security could actually lead to conflict with its opponents.

In 2001, however, Mearsheimer openly challenged Walt's concept in his groundbreaking book, *The Tragedy of Great Power Politics*.[7] This text set Mearsheimer apart from Waltz, Walt, and other realists by developing the theory of offensive realism,* according to which states will try to maximize their power relative to one another—rather than simply obtain just enough power to maintain security.

NOTES

1 Thucydides, *The History Of The Peloponnesian War*, trans. Rex Warner (New York: Penguin Classics; rev. edn, 1954).

2 Thucydides, *History of the Peloponnesian War*, trans. Thomas Crowley (Auckland: Floating Library, 2008), 568.

3   Hans Morgenthau, *Politics Among Nations* (New York: Knopf, 1948).

4   Robert Keohane and Joseph Nye, *Power and Interdependence* (New York: Little, Brown, 1977).

5   John J. Mearsheimer, *Conventional Deterrence* (Ithica, NY: Cornell University Press, 1983).

6   Stephen M. Walt, *The Origins of Alliances* (Ithica, NY: Cornell University Press, 1987).

7   John J. Mearsheimer, *The Tragedy of Great Power Politics* (New York: W.W. Norton & Company, 2001).

MODULE 4
THE AUTHOR'S CONTRIBUTION

KEY POINTS

- Kenneth Waltz wanted to find a theory to explain why, even when governments and leaders change, relations among countries tend to remain the same. His answer was this: what matters is not so much the domestic politics of countries, but rather the chaotic international system in which they operate.

- Waltz was strongly influenced by the French sociologist Émile Durkheim,* who came to the same conclusion about society—that the features of the system as a whole are more important that the features of any individuals in it.

- Waltz is the founder of neorealism,* which claims to have a more scientific approach to international relations than the classical realist* school of thought that it grew out of.

Author's Aims

When Kenneth Waltz decided to write *Theory of International Politics*, his aim was to find the factors that have been constant in politics, across all of human history, in order to determine why war persists despite every possible combination of states and statesmen. In doing so, his text transformed the way scholars study international relations by introducing a new, ground-breaking theoretical model that sought to apply a scientific method to the classical realist* model.

The aim of the text, according to Waltz, was to create a theory that could explain the following problem: changes in international outcomes are typically the result of changes in "actors"—the leaders and governments in charge of countries. Yet outcomes often remain

29

> **❝** It is not possible to understand world politics simply by looking inside of states. If the aims, policies, and actions of states become matters of exclusive attention or even of central concern, then we are forced back to the descriptive level; and from simple descriptions no valid generalizations can logically be drawn. **❞**
>
> Kenneth Waltz, *Theory of International Politics*

similar even when actors change. By "international outcomes," Waltz was referring mainly to "high politics"*—the actions that governments take toward other governments. Waltz made a point of emphasizing that all actions by countries occur in what he calls the "brooding shadow of violence" that hangs over countries in an anarchical* international system[1]—one where there is no leader or authority to make countries act fairly or correctly.

At the time Waltz wrote *Theory*, most theorists of international relations studied state-level factors, meaning they looked at the domestic politics of countries (which Waltz referred to as "unit-level factors") to try to explain international politics.[2]

Waltz, however, felt that domestic politics was not the key factor influencing how countries acted toward one another. It was the anarchic international system itself that accounted for the patterns of state action— patterns repeated over and over for millennia. His focus on the international system, rather than the states, accounts for how Waltz's theory "explains why war recurs, and indicates some of the conditions that make war more or less likely; but does not predict the outbreak of particular wars."[3] By focusing on the international system instead of the states themselves in *Theory*, Waltz is able to draw positivist* conclusions about state action, which means he identifies laws of politics based on observation, similar to the way that a scientist might come up with laws of physics. This was a new and distinct approach to the study of international relations.

Approach

Waltz takes a scientific approach in *Theory*, focusing on two main theoretical issues: 1) realism* and 2) the structure of the international system. Specifically, Waltz's theory contains many standard realist ideas: the international system is chaotic; states are the main actors in the international system; and states naturally compete with one another in a quest for power. Crucial for Waltz's theory is the idea that security is the single greatest concern of states, leading them to be naturally suspicious of other states' motivations and concerned mainly with relative gains*—often sacrificing absolute gains* if there is a risk another state will gain more. In other words, they want to keep the balance of power in their favor above all else.

Waltz developed his theory of neorealism after reading the sociologist Émile Durkheim's* *The Division of Labour in Society*, which argued that the behavior of units within systems was defined by the features of the system itself, rather than by any particular feature of the units.[4] It was this line of reasoning that led Waltz to conclude that the major causes of war were to be found in the relationship among the states in the anarchic international system, rather than in the states or their leaders.[5] States, according to Waltz's theory, are "undifferentiated units" or, in other words, units that are in a sense all the same. All perform the same functions, like providing security, though with varying success based on their individual military capabilities, which is determined by "countable" things such as the numbers of guns, soldiers, and bombs.

By rethinking realism and focusing on the structure of the international system, Waltz in effect became the father of the neorealist school of international relations.[6]

Contribution in Context

Kenneth Waltz's *Theory* is the founding text of the neorealist school of thought, making it entirely original. Certainly, Waltz drew on other

scholars for inspiration, like the classical realist scholar Hans Morgenthau*
and the sociologist Émile Durkheim, when writing his text. Waltz's
intellectual roots came from classical realism. Morgenthau summarized
the central outlook of the classical realists in his 1948 text, *Politics Among
Nations:* "[All] politics ... is governed by objective laws which have their
roots in human nature."[7] However, to Waltz, classical realism was an
"agent-driven" theory and more of a philosophy than a science. To
overcome these limitations, Waltz simply applied a scientific method to
Morgenthau's realist ideas, which led to his theory of neorealism.

As noted above, Émile Durkheim's *The Division of Labor in Society*
(1893) heavily influenced Waltz's theory of neorealism. It convinced
him that studies of international relations focused far too much on the
behavior of individual states and not enough on the features of the
international system. Waltz's application of Durkheim's sociological
ideas to international relations theory presented a groundbreaking
approach to how scholars examine the interactions of states.

NOTES

1   Kenneth Waltz, *Theory of International Politics* (Reading: Addison Wesley, 1979), 102.

2   Waltz, *Theory*, 60.

3   Waltz, *Theory*, 69.

4   Émile Durkheim, *The Division of Labour in Society*, trans. George Simpson (New York: Free Press, 1964), 257.

5   Waltz, Theory, 99.

6   Ken Booth, "The Darwin of International Relations," *Foreign Policy*, May 15, 2013, accessed December 6, 2013, http://www.foreignpolicy.com/ articles/2013/05/15/requiem_for_a_realist_kenneth_waltz?page=0,4.

7   Hans Morgenthau, *Politics Among Nations* (New York: McGraw Hill, 1979), 4.

SECTION 2
IDEAS

MODULE 5
MAIN IDEAS

KEY POINTS

- Kenneth Waltz's *Theory* states that the anarchy* of the world order pushes countries to focus on their security against other countries. In the end, Waltz claims, countries are all the same in this respect; only their respective military strengths differ.

- He and other authors had raised this idea earlier; in *Theory*, Waltz develops it more fully.

- Waltz wrote *Theory* for an academic audience, using highly technical language and assuming that readers had a familiarity with international relations theory.

Key Themes

The main aim of Kenneth Waltz's *Theory of International Politics* is "to examine theories of international politics and approaches to the subject matter that make some claim to being theoretically important … to construct a theory of international politics that remedies the defects of present theories … and to examine some applications of the theory constructed."[1]

To do so, Waltz sought to provide a new theory of international relations that answers the question: "If changes in international outcomes are linked directly to changes in actors, how can one account for similarities of outcome [such as the occurrence of war or the emergences of balances of power] that persist or recur even as actors vary?"[2]

The central theme of *Theory* is the concept of realism,* which assumes that the international system is anarchic,* states seek power

> **66** In a self-help system each of the units spends a
> portion of its effort, not in forwarding its own good, but
> in providing the means of protecting itself against others
> ... When faced with the problem of mutual gain, states
> that feel insecure must ask how the gain will be divided.
> They are compelled to ask not 'Will both of us gain?'
> but 'Who will gain more?' **99**
>
> Kenneth Waltz, *Theory of International Politics*

over one another, "great powers" typically emerge, and, finally, that politics between countries often involves war. At the same time, Waltz's text has a strong secondary theme of criticism of the classical realist theory, which he accuses of reducing* the international system into an overly simplified model. In the book, he says that previous studies of international relations tended to focus far too much on the behavior of individual states and not enough on the features of the international system.

Waltz argues that the anarchy of the international system affects how states act. Those that do not give a high priority to security against other states do not survive. Countries are therefore conditioned to maximize their security against others; it is a case of survival of the fittest. Waltz believes the laws of politics are similar to laws of physics: states can be understood as "billiard balls," differentiated from one another only by military capability. In this model, the actions of countries are determined by their relative sizes and positions in the system—just as the relative sizes and positions of two or more billiard balls would affect their movements on a billiard table.

Exploring the Ideas

Even as he is critical of the shortcomings of international relations realism, Waltz maintains the use of key realist ideas. For instance, he sees the international system as leaderless (consistent with the idea of anarchy), where actors (states) seek to maximize their own national interests (their power relative to other states) in order to ensure their own survival. In other words, the international system creates a situation whereby states are cynical actors determined to improve their situation vis-à-vis other states. Crucial for Waltz's theory is the realist idea that security is the single greatest concern of states, leading them to be naturally suspicious of each other's motivations.

The idea that anarchy can be thought of as a force shaping politics between and among countries is not entirely original to *Theory*. The American philosopher Mortimer Adler* had raised this idea in *How to Think About War and Peace*, published 1944. In that book, Adler wrote that peace would not be possible "until international anarchy is replaced by world government."[3] Waltz reflected this notion in his previous work, *Man, The State, and War*, published in 1959,[4] when he said that a "prescription for peace" will only be effective in preventing war if the establishment of a world government would turn the international system from anarchy to hierarchy*—a system of authority that could make countries act in a certain way.

Waltz's core concern in *Theory*, therefore, was to adapt those previous ideas into a scientific theory of state action.

Language and Expression

When Kenneth Waltz wrote *Theory,* his intended audience was chiefly academic—what he refers to in the text as "students of politics."[5] This is immediately clear from Waltz's focus on theory, an approach that would interest few people outside the academic world. His central concern was to construct "a theory of international politics that remedies the defects of present theories"—in other words, a new model that is applicable in real life.[6]

Waltz's expectation that his audience would be primarily academic gave him the freedom to assume significant knowledge of political theory on the part of his readers. For instance, in the second and third chapters, he is able to go directly into criticism of existing theories of international politics, such as neocolonialism* (the theory that capitalism motivates nations to build empires), without wasting time explaining the historical context or the content of the theory. Given this, the layman would consider the language that he uses to deliver his arguments quite sophisticated.

Still, Waltz structures the text in an easily understood manner. He breaks it down into nine chapters, organized according to his three objectives. The first four chapters focus on other "theories of international politics and approaches to the subject matter that make some claim to being theoretically important."[7] For instance, in the first chapter, Waltz lays out his definition of theory and, in the next three chapters, he critiques the major theoretical models of international relations, particularly classical realism. He describes it as reductionist*— that is, as oversimplified to the detriment of accuracy

In the fifth chapter, Waltz addresses his second objective of constructing "a theory of international politics that remedies the defects of present theories."[8] Then, in the final four chapters, he lays out the theoretical basis for his approach—neorealism—through discussions about how the world order is a type of anarchy, the balance of power politics, and the structural causes of economic and military conflicts. In the final chapter, Waltz uses practical examples to show how his theory applies to real events, drawing on examples ranging from competition between car manufacturers to the American war in Vietnam.*

NOTES

1   Kenneth Waltz, *Theory of International Politics* (Reading: Addison Wesley, 1979), 1.

2   Waltz, *Theory*, 65.

3   Mortimer Adler, *How to Think About War and Peace* (New York: Simon and Schuster, 1944), 81.

4   Kenneth Waltz, *Man, the State, and War: A Theoretical Analysis* (New York: Columbia University Press, 1959), 68.

5   Waltz, *Theory*, 4.

6   Waltz, *Theory*, 1.

7   Waltz, *Theory*, 1.

8   Waltz, *Theory*, 1.

SECONDARY IDEAS

KEY POINTS

- Inspired by the French sociologist Émile Durkheim's* systems theory, Waltz overturned the study of international relations to shift the focus to the system as a whole and how it affects the actions of individual countries.

- Waltz's positivist* approach suggested that "laws" could be determined for international politics, just as they can be for physics, through an examination of real-world events.

- The most overlooked part of the text is Waltz's discussion of "metatheory" (i.e., a theory of theories), where he talks about the difference between laws and theories.

Other Ideas

The second major element of Kenneth Waltz's *Theory of International Politics* was his desire to rethink how the field is studied.

In the book, Waltz criticizes other theorists for failing to adopt a scientific approach to the study of international affairs and for trying to account for too much. Part of the problem was that these other scholars tended to use the language of scientific theory, whereby international outcomes ("dependent variables") are thought to result from domestic conditions ("independent variables"). In other words, they said that the state of relations between and among countries—cooperation, war, or something in between—depends on what kind of governments those countries have but for Waltz, this is not true. He argues that these other scholars were using scientific-sounding terms too loosely, without proper scientific rigor.[1]

Seeing classical realism as an insufficient theoretical model of

> ❝ A theory is a picture, mentally formed, of a bounded realm or domain of activity. A theory is a depiction of the organization of a domain and of the connections among its parts. ❞
>
> Kenneth Waltz, *Theory of International Politics*

analysis, Waltz sought to revolutionize the discipline by formulating a truly scientific approach to the study of international relations. To do so, he adapted Émile Durkheim's,* "systems theory" to the study of international relations, which allowed him to develop a model that focused on the international system as a whole and how it impacted the interactions of states.[2]

From Waltz's point of view, by combining the central elements of realist theory with the positivist,* (that is, roughly, scientific) elements of Durkheim's systems theory, he was able to develop a new theory of international relations that focused on the international system as a whole and the distribution of capabilities among states, each of which has the main aim of continued survival in the face of threats or competition from other states.

Exploring the Ideas

In order to understand Waltz's text, a brief explanation of its relationship to positivism is necessary.

Positivism is a philosophy of science based on the idea that people receive information from their sensory experience (things seen, heard, and otherwise verified), and they can use that sensory experience to create "laws." For example, one might sense that apples drop when they lose their attachment to trees and, in sensing that, come up with the law of gravity. Positivism, as applied to social sciences, believes that certain laws govern the social world, just as other laws govern the physical one.

Waltz's theory had two major points in common with positivism.

First, neorealism,* attempted to derive "laws" of international politics akin to laws of physics, and second, Waltz believed that concepts like anarchy,* are observable and objective—in other words, that anarchy has a clear meaning and can be expected when certain conditions are in place. However, while Waltz's theory had a lot in common with positivism, the two approaches differed in some ways. Waltz felt the positivists relied too much on their observations of the actions of individual countries and were not capable of stepping back and considering the wider picture of the international system as a whole. He wrote "to construct a theory, we must abstract from reality … [and] leave aside most of what we see and experience."[3]

Overlooked

The most overlooked aspect of *Theory of International Politics* is Waltz's discussion of "metatheory" or the "theory of theory": his stand-alone theory of how to make a theory. Throughout his first chapter, "Laws and Theories," Waltz analyzes in detail the nature of laws and theories. He explains that a "law is based not simply on a relation that has been found, but on one that has been found repeatedly."[4] Theories, in contrast, are not ideas that people can discover through examination of facts or the accumulation of hypotheses about laws of action. Instead, theories are statements that people use to explain laws.[5]

One problem that Waltz identified with previous theories of international relations, like realism,* and liberalism,,* is that they rely on what is known as an "inductivist,* illusion"—which means they attempt to come up with theories "through the accumulation of more and more data and the examination of more and more cases." In the end, as Waltz observes in *Theory*, "We will simply end up having more and more data and larger sets of correlation"—but no objective truth.[6]

"A theory is a picture," Waltz writes, "mentally formed, of a bounded realm or domain of activity … and the connections among its parts."[7] By "bounded realm," he means that there could never be a theory of politics in general, because the different "domestic" and "international" realms are bounded, or roped off, and governed by different laws. Waltz did not believe that theory represented reality perfectly; rather, a theory explains reality as it operates within a "bounded" realm. In other words, Waltz intended for people to view his theory as an analytical device, not as a description of the real world.

Unfortunately, the significance of the theoretical model that he introduces in the rest of the text overshadows his analysis of laws and theories, and his warning of their limits in describing reality. In 2009, however, the Danish international relations scholar Ole Wæver published an article, "Theory of Theory," that argued that Waltz's followers, the so-called Waltzians, had misrepresented much of his work. As Wæver observed, "The book's grand success owed much to being widely accepted as setting a new standard for 'theory' in the discipline. Given all of this, it is surprising how little attention has been paid to what Waltz says about the nature of theory."

In particular, Wæver found that Waltz's followers had ignored his warnings that theory is meant to be used only as an analytical device, and that to apply it to real-world events would be to distort reality.[8]

NOTES

1   Kenneth Waltz, *Theory of International Politics* (Reading: Addison Wesley, 1979), 65.

2   Waltz, *Theory*, 61.

3   Waltz, *Theory*, 68.

4   Waltz, *Theory*, 1.

5   Waltz, *Theory*, 5.

6   Waltz, *Theory*, 4.

7   Waltz, *Theory*, 8.

8   Ole Wæver, "Waltz's Theory of Theory," *International Politics* 23, no. 2 (2009): 204–5.

MODULE 7
ACHIEVEMENT

KEY POINTS

- *Theory of International Politics* presents a scientific theory of how one might conduct an analysis of international relations without making assumptions about particular people or states. To this end, Kenneth Waltz was very successful

- The relative simplicity of the high-stakes international environment during the Cold War* tended to reinforce Waltz's abstract reasoning. It was a zero-sum* competition: one state's loss was another's victory.

- In a post-Cold War international environment, the influence of Waltz's approach, neorealism,* has waned due to its limited applicability.

Assessing the Argument

When Kenneth Waltz set out to write *Theory of International Politics*, he had three primary objectives:

- to examine theories of international politics and other scholarly approaches considered to be important;
- to construct a theory of international politics that remedies the defects of previous theories;
- to offer examples of the application of his new theory to real-world situations.[1]

To that end, Waltz was very successful, as evidenced by *Theory's* status as a basic text for the study of international relations and his reputation as the founder of a major school of thought with countless followers.[2]

> **❝** Intellectually speaking, we are all Waltz's subjects, whether we be loyal disciples, friendly critics, or rebellious opponents: the discipline defines itself in relation to the authority of his work. **❞**
> Ken Booth, *The King of Thought*

Perhaps the most valuable aspect of Waltz's theory was its ability to create a science out of the international relations approach known as realism.* Waltz did this by rigorously applying positivist* methods to it—in other words, by basing his theories on observations and testing them through experimentation and further observations. For Waltz, that meant coming up with reliable, enduring laws—more like laws of physics than models in social science—of how countries act on the international scene. He concluded that war was a natural and certain outcome of international anarchy,* for example, because states are naturally competitive—seeking power, influence, resources, and so on. To this day, that conclusion holds true.

Achievement in Context

Theory was most clearly relevant in the context of the Cold War. Writing in the late 1970s, Waltz based his theory of international politics on the most important common features that he observed, such as competition among countries, the balance of power between two great powers,* the outbreak of war, and the formation of alliances. His theory rested on a number of key ideas. For instance, Waltz believed that, in terms of relations among countries, all states are basically alike, only "great power" politics matters, and domestic factors do not matter.[3] All of these notions were evident in the behavior of countries during the Cold War.

Waltz is considered to have "freed" international relations from its status as just a division of history or political theory and turned it into its own, theoretically rigorous discipline—one that could be applied to the real world.[4] Throughout the 1980s, a debate raged about the conclusions of *Theory*, with Waltz arguing that international anarchy meant that states naturally compete and the political theorist Robert Keohane* and other neoliberal institutionalists arguing that international anarchy does not rule out the possibility of cooperation—especially given the existence of international institutions to allow nations to reap the benefits of cooperation.

When the Cold War came to an abrupt end in 1991, it was suddenly obvious that the bipolar, zero-sum* nature of international affairs (where a loss for one of the world's two superpowers was a gain for the other) had been replaced by system that was unipolar* (with one remaining superpower) or multipolar* (with several superpowers). As a result, the global balance of power was now less important as a force in international affairs than, for example, influences extending across several borders. Those might include interventions in "failed" states, such as the Yugoslav Wars in the 1990s,* or the actions of transnational terrorist groups, such as al-Qaeda* or the Islamic State of Iraq and Syria/the Levant (ISIS or ISIL).*

Given that neorealism was based on the actions of countries, Waltz's theory struggled to adapt to such new post-Cold War sources of turmoil without sacrificing its core ideas. As a result, the influence of the neorealist theoretical model has declined somewhat, although the text remains a key starting point for students learning the basics of international relations theory.

Limitations

Waltz intended the text to be a viewed as model for analyzing international affairs. However, its greatest weakness is that he had expected that the international conditions of the Cold War were natural and would continue beyond the end of that conflict, but the post-Cold War period has proved that idea false.

For example, Waltz assumed that states were the only actors in global politics and that "great power" states, like the United States and Soviet Union,* were the only important actors from that group.[5] He also assumed that in an anarchical international system, there would always be competition between states. However, in a post-Cold War context, these ideas seem outdated. World politics is now taken up, in no small part, by the actions of transnational terrorist groups, against whom states have tended to cooperate. This means that Waltz's neorealist* analysis is mostly limited to a Cold War context.

After the end of the Cold War, discussions about international relations theory took a "post-positivist turn."* This new direction rejected the discipline's earlier claims to be based on scientific principles. Starting in the 1990s, new types of analysis, like critical theory* and constructivism,* emerged and took aim at both neorealism's methods and conclusions. The constructivist theorist Friedrich Kratochwil,* for example, argued that neorealism's focus on "giving greater precision, depth, and above all, scientific respectability" to international relations, closes the discipline off from alternative ideas.

Treating international relations as a "hard" science with fixed laws, Kratochwil suggested, only limits the number of questions scholars can ask, and thereby reduces the whole discipline's chance of finding valid answers.[6] In an ironic turn, the theory that set out to challenge the reductionism* of previous theories—by claiming that their oversimplification of older theories made them miss the forest for the trees—was now viewed as being reductionist itself.

NOTES

1   Kenneth Waltz, *Theory of International Politics* (Reading: Addison Wesley, 1979), 1.

2   Ken Booth, "The Darwin of International Relations," *Foreign Policy*, May 15, 2013, accessed December 6, 2013, http://www.foreignpolicy.com/articles/2013/05/15/requiem_for_a_realist_kenneth_waltz?page=0,4.

3   Waltz, *Theory*, 99.

4   Michael Williams, "Waltz, Realism, and Democracy," *International Relations* 23, no. 3 (2009): 338.

5   Waltz, *Theory*, 172.

6   Friedrich Kratochwil, "The Embarrassment of Changes: Neorealism as the Science of Realpolitik without Politics," *Review of International Studies* 19, no. 1 (1993): 63–4.

MODULE 8
PLACE IN THE AUTHOR'S WORK

KEY POINTS

- *Man, The State, and War*, Waltz's first book, was his initial attack on the weaknesses of the realist* approach. It took him another two decades to refine his ideas before publishing his most famous work, *Theory of International Politics*.

- Over time, Waltz changed some of his opinions, most notably on nuclear weapons, which he came to see as a stabilizing force.

- The neorealist* approach that Waltz inspired lost some of its relevance after the end of the Cold War,* but it remains intellectually important and *Theory of International Politics* is still considered to be one of the most significant international relations texts of the twentieth century.

Positioning

Theory of International Politics is, without question, Kenneth Waltz's most famous work. Indeed, as the first major book on the neorealist school of thought, it is one of the most influential texts of international relations in the twentieth century.

Within Waltz's work, *Theory* was published in the middle of his career, as a follow-up to his first book, *Man, the State, and War*, an expanded version of his PhD thesis that he published in 1959. While studying economics and political philosophy at Columbia University, Waltz became inspired by the work of his supervisor, William T. R. Fox,* who famously coined the terms "superpower"* and "bipolar"* in his 1944 text, *The Super-Powers: The United States, Britain, and the*

48

> ❝ There is a constant possibility of war in a world in which there are two or more states each seeking to promote a set of interests and having no agency above them upon which they can rely for protection. ❞
>
> Kenneth Waltz, *Man, The State, and War*

Soviet Union—Their Responsibility for Peace.[1] In that work, Fox described the nature of the relationship between the Soviet Union* and the United States.

Waltz's *Man, The State, and War*, like the later *Theory of International Politics*, was an influential text for those who study international relations. His primary goal was to answer the question "How can the major causes of war be determined, and how can war be predicted and controlled?" In looking at the means to answer these questions, Waltz found that the main theory at the time, classical realism,* left him unsatisfied. Not surprisingly, soon after *Man, The State, and War*'s publication, a colleague asked Waltz, "What's going to be the sequel?"[2] Though it took him 20 years, Waltz developed *Theory* in order to address the scholarly issues not adequately answered that he first identified in *Man, The State, and War*.

Integration

Throughout Waltz's career, from his studies at Columbia University after World War II* through to his death in 2013, his primary focus was how to best understand the international system.

In *Man, The State, and War*, Waltz concluded that the frequency of war is caused by the state of anarchy in the international system. The same focus can be seen in *Theory*, which sought to develop a theoretical model to analyze international affairs. While his first text was a significant contribution to the field, *Theory* is considered to be the most important and influential work of Waltz's career, and the one that defined the school of neorealism. *Theory* introduced a more scientific account of international politics and a school of thought that many prominent international relations theorists, such as John Mearsheimer* and Stephen Walt,* have carried on since then.

Understandably, as Waltz's career advanced, he spent much of his time refining and defending his neorealist approach in the face of growing criticism.[3] However, he was not entirely rigid on the question of nuclear weapons, and his views underwent significant shifts over time.

For instance, in *Theory*, Waltz argues that "the perennial [long-standing] forces of politics are more important than the new military technology" in shaping state behavior.[4] Nevertheless, when Waltz published his 1995 work, *The Spread of Nuclear Weapons*, it was clear that he had changed his position, arguing instead that nuclear weapons had deeply changed the international system because they made the destruction of an entire country possible. Ironically, they were more effective at preventing conflict than anything that had ever existed before.[5]

Significance

According to scholars of international relations, Waltz's *Theory* has undoubtedly had a tremendous impact on its field. Not only did Waltz introduce a new, groundbreaking theoretical approach, but his work was also key to establishing the field of international relations as a separate academic discipline.

Despite the text's original significance as a major force in international relations, however, neorealism's influence has faded somewhat following the end of the Cold War. In a new situation, with the United States as the only remaining superpower and terrorism a major concern since the terrorist attacks on the World Trade Center in New York on September 11, 2001, "scholarly and public attention turned to a new range of political problems to which neorealism was irrelevant."[6]

Nevertheless, *Theory of International Politics* has enjoyed enormous lasting influence because it set the stage for more nuanced methods of analysis. As the international politics scholar Chris Brown* observed, "Contemporary [international relations] is fixated on *Theory of International Politics.* Not only was Realism revitalized by this book, but also anti-Realists have felt obliged to respond to its arguments."[7]

Brown is not alone in his praise of Waltz. Mearsheimer once wrote that Waltz was "the most important international relations theorist of the past half century." Stephen Walt, meanwhile, said that he was "the pre-eminent international relations theorist of the post-World War II era." The neoliberal* theorist Robert Keohane,* Waltz's ideological opponent, called him "the pre-eminent theorist of international politics of his generation."[8] By the time Waltz died in 2013, he had established a reputation as one of leading scholars of international relations.

NOTES

1   William T. R. Fox, *The Super-Powers: The United States, Britain, and the Soviet Union — Their Responsibility for Peace* (New York: Harcourt, Brace and Company, 1944).

2   Harry Kriesler, *Theory and International Politics: Conversation with Kenneth Waltz*, accessed October 16, 2013, http://globetrotter.berkeley.edu/people3/Waltz/.

3   See Kenneth Waltz, "A Response to Critics," in *Neorealism and Its Critics*, ed. Robert Keohane (New York: Columbia University Press, 1986), 322–46.

4   Kenneth Waltz, *Theory of International Politics* (Reading: Addison Wesley, 1979), 173.

5   Scott Sagan and Kenneth Waltz, *The Spread of Nuclear Weapons: A Debate* (New York: W.W. Norton, 1995).

6   Richard Ned Lebow, "Classical Realism," in *International Relations Theories*, ed. Tim Dunne, Milja Kurki, and Steve Smith (Oxford: Oxford University Press, 2007), 53.

7   Chris Brown and Kirsten Ainley, *Understanding International Relations* (London: Palgrave MacMillan, 2005), 40.

8   William Rooke, "Great IR Thinkers: Kenneth Waltz," *International Relations and Security Network*, October 6, 2011, accessed January 14, 2015, http://isnblog.ethz.ch/international-relations/great-ir-thinkers-kenneth-waltz.

SECTION 3
IMPACT

THE FIRST RESPONSES

KEY POINTS

- Those people who followed the liberal* school of thought in international relations criticized Kenneth Waltz's *Theory of International Politics* for failing to account for the reality of cooperation among rational states. Constructivists,* meanwhile, who emphasize the way that societies determine international relations, criticized his work for assuming that all states act rationally.

- Waltz responded to both views by claiming that the critics misunderstood his theory and what it was trying to do: to develop a broad-based theory to cover a wide range of possibilities

- After the end of the Cold War,* Waltz's neorealism* was increasingly seen as too one-sided—focusing only on a country's security aims. A new trend, neoclassical realism,* saw the truth in a compromise between Waltz and his critics.

Criticism

Criticism of Kenneth Waltz's neorealist* *Theory of International Politics* came from two quarters: neoliberals* and critical theorists.*

Broadly speaking, critics took issue with neorealism's dream to be a "grand theory." The neoliberal theorist Robert Keohane* rejected neorealism's claim that one should expect all states, regardless of their individual politics or character, to act similarly in a given international situation, writing, "Even if interests are taken as given, the attempt to predict outcomes from interests and power [exclusively] leads to ambiguities and incorrect predictions."[1] To him, Waltz's idea that

> ❝ We need to respond to the questions that realism poses but fails to answer: how can order be created out of anarchy without superordinate power; how can peaceful change occur? ❞
> Robert Keohane, "Theory of World Politics: Structural Realism and Beyond"

countries always want to maximize power was problematic and presented neorealists with the following dilemma: either they maintain this error and fail to take into account the idea that states can have "competing goals, some of which would be generated by the internal social, political, and economic characteristics of the countries concerned," or they accept that these competing factors are important and reduce neorealism to "the status of a partial, incomplete theory."[2]

A second source of criticism of *Theory* came from critical theorists,* whose work questioned many of the very assumptions about knowledge on which the social sciences were founded. The British theorist Richard Ashley,* for example, took issue with neorealism's similarity to the hard sciences and its focus on structure, writing that "far from expanding international political discourse, [neorealism] excludes all standpoints that would expose the limits of the given order of things."[3] Ashley also attacked Waltz's take on positivism* (his approach to working from observable evidence and practically testing theory) and neorealism's surface resemblance to natural science. By studying international relations as a natural science, Ashley argued, Waltz "profoundly [limits] the range of possibilities that theory can contemplate if it is to find acceptance as an objective scientific theory."[4] Positivism, argued Ashley, tends to produce theories that do not at all reflect social values, emphasizing mathematical rationality, thereby making Waltz's work a "theory masked as method."[5]

With the end of the Cold War* in 1991 and the collapse of the bipolar world order (a system of two superpowers confronting each other), neorealism and neoliberalism appeared to become obsolete. They were theories designed to account for a bipolar international structure.

According to the Danish political theorist Ole Wæver,* the two theories "no longer [lacked any common features] … on the contrary, they shared a rationalist research program [that is, they were based on reason rather than emotions], a conception of science, [and] a shared willingness to operate on the premise of anarchy."[6] In that vein, the debate began to emphasize critical and constructivist positions, which accounted for the role of different societies in the formulation of foreign policy, while increasingly grouping together neorealism and neoliberalism, which both focused on a bipolar world, as antiquated.

Responses

Because *Theory* was central to the theoretical debate between neorealism and neoliberalism (the first seeing ruthless competition as the natural state of affairs between countries and the latter seeing cooperation), it generated a great deal of interest—both critical and approving. Robert Keohane's edited volume, *Neorealism and Its Critics* (1986), captured the debate, featuring the views of a range of scholars of international relations, including Waltz.[7] The text gave Waltz an opportunity to respond to the challenges that the neoliberals had put forward.

In that book of essays, Waltz played down the differences between the two theories, suggesting they had a difference of "emphasis," but little basic disagreement. He noted that both theories shared similar beliefs, especially the notion that states act rationally in an anarchic* world order.[8] However, whereas Keohane had a wider view of state interests, including issues vital to both the survival of the state and the welfare of the state, Waltz focused on state survival.

In response to Ashley's critique, Waltz wrote, "Ashley's main objection seems to be that I did not write a theory of domestic politics … That is so because I essayed an international political theory and not a domestic one. Not everything can go into one book and not everything can go into one theory."[9] However, Waltz's response to Ashley also drifted away from the theoretical toward the personal: "I find [Ashley] difficult to deal with. Reading his essay is like entering a maze. I never know quite where I am or how to get out."[10]

Conflict and Consensus

Despite the debate surrounding Waltz's theory, he did not change his views, but instead hardened his position in the face of challenges. Waltz also faced new challenges from scholars from a new school of thought called neoclassical realism. Emerging in the 1990s, its followers claim that state action can be explained with reference to both structural factors (such as the distribution of capabilities between states) and agent-driven factors (such as the ambitions of countries' leaders). To them, the problem with Waltz's analysis was that he defined power narrowly, largely in terms of military capability. Neoclassical realists turned back to the classical realist* work of scholars such as Hans Morgenthau* in order to capture the "human," as well as scientific, side of politics.

For example, the American theorist Richard Ned Lebow,* a neoclassical realist, challenged Waltz's claim that neorealism continued to be useful after the Cold War. He wrote, "Waltz now insists that the international system remains bipolar even after the breakup of the Soviet Union.* His depiction of the post–Cold War world as bipolar is strikingly at odds with the views of other prominent realists. More to the point, it cannot be derived from the definition of power in Waltz's *Theory*."[11] While neoclassical realists recognized that neorealism did a good job describing security competition between states, the problem was that it emphasized only one aspect of international relations at the expense of other, potentially more useful lines of inquiry.

Faced with this new wave of criticism, Waltz countered by insisting that neorealism's core would remain relevant and useful as long as the international system remained the same. For instance, in a 2000 article,

"Structural Realism After the Cold War," Waltz suggested that the end of the Cold War meant a new type of international anarchy,* rather than a change of the system from anarchy to hierarchy.*[12]

NOTES

1   Robert Keohane, "Theory of World Politics: Structural Realism and Beyond," in *Neorealism and Its Critics*, ed. Robert Keohane (New York: Columbia University Press, 1986), 190.

2   Keohane, "Theory," 174.

3   Richard Ashley, "The Poverty of Neorealism," in *Neorealism and Its Critics*, ed. Robert Keohane (New York: Columbia University Press, 1986), 268.

4   Ashley, "Poverty," 285.

5   Ashley, "Poverty," 285.

6   Ole Wæver, "The Rise and Fall of the Inter-Paradigm Debate," in *International Theory: Positivism and Beyond*, ed. Steve Smith, Ken Booth, and Marysia Zalewski (Cambridge: Cambridge University Press, 1996), 163.

7   Robert Keohane, ed., *Neorealism and Its Critics* (New York: Columbia University Press, 1986).

8   Kenneth Waltz, "A Response to Critics," in *Neorealism and Its Critics*, ed. Robert Keohane (New York: Columbia University Press, 1986), 330.

9   Waltz, "Response," 339.

10 Waltz, "Response," 337.

11 Richard Ned Lebow, "The Long Peace, the End of the Cold War, and the Failure of Realism," *International Organization* 48, no. 2 (1994): 254.

12 Kenneth Waltz, "Structural Realism After the Cold War," *International Security* 25, no. 1 (2000): 5.

MODULE 10
THE EVOLVING DEBATE

KEY POINTS

- *Theory* drove a shift in international relations theory from "philosophy" to "science," but this shift has been disputed since the early 1990s.

- Although neorealism* continues as a school of thought to this day, the end of the Cold War* weakened its appeal and helped to inspire a modified theory: neoclassical realism.*

- Recent trends have added new dimensions to Waltz's neorealism. For example, in a 2001 book, the neorealist scholar John Mearsheimer* introduced the idea of offensive realism.*

Uses and Problems

Following the publication of Kenneth Waltz's *Theory of International Politics*, a major shift occurred in the study of international relations. Waltz's work was at the very center of a major re-evaluation of the core of the field, with both Waltz's followers and opponents jockeying to position themselves within the emerging debate.

The scientific revolution that Waltz created by publishing *Theory* helped define two "great debates" within the discipline. The first debate occurred in the 1980s and centered on differences between supporters of neorealism* (like Waltz) and supporters of neoliberalism (such as Robert Keohane).* Both theories viewed positivism* (roughly, basing theories on observed facts) as central to their methodology and agreed on the core belief that states were the primary actors of international affairs. They also agreed that states were naturally rational and that anarchy was the defining feature of

> **❝** The two paradigms [realism* and liberalism*] had different strengths, there were things better explained by the one, and others dealt better with the other. And more importantly, there was no way to prove one or the other right. Realists and [liberals]... saw different realities. **❞**
>
> Ole Wæver, "The Rise and Fall of the Inter-Paradigm Debate"

international politics. They disagreed, however, on their conclusions.

Neoliberals, for example, argued that cooperation and competition were both possible results of interaction between countries because states were as interested in welfare as they were in security. For neorealists, however, only competition was possible.[1] In that sense, *Theory*'s scientific leaning influenced both sides of the great debate.

Waltz's text was not as central to the second debate, which was, in broad terms, between positivists (that is, neoliberals and neorealists) and a group identifying themselves as post-positivists,* who believe that the background or values of a researcher can affect their observations and cloud their judgments.

The Danish theorist Ole Wæver* first identified this second great debate in an article of 1996, where he characterized the positivist "alliance" of neorealists and neoliberals as the "Neo-Neo Synthesis."[2] Post-positivists, like the German political theorist Alexander Wendt,* rejected the beliefs of the positivists as artificially narrow, and criticized their claim that international relations is a science. In doing so, he argued, they limited the kinds of questions the discipline could ask. Wendt challenged Waltz's belief that anarchy* naturally conditioned states to be competitive, and he suggested that states choose to compete in anarchy, thereby "making" anarchy a competitive system. States, according to Wendt, could just as easily choose to cooperate and make anarchy a cooperative system.[3]

The rise of post-positivist theory and the change in the nature of international politics have both contributed to the decline of neorealism as a leading theory.

Schools of Thought

The most direct outcome of Waltz's text was the establishment of neorealism as a school of thought within the field of international relations. Toward the end of the Cold War, neorealism proved to be an attractive and distinctive model due to its positivist methods. Yet as narrow and supposedly similar to science as it was, neorealism was later criticized for having numerous beliefs about the international system that no longer seemed valid after the end of the Cold War in the early 1990s.

At a basic level, neorealism assumes that competition between countries is a natural, and indeed unavoidable, outcome of states dealing with one another under anarchy. While neorealism's importance as a theoretical model has declined since the end of the Cold War, that has not stopped Waltz's followers, like John Mearsheimer and Stephen Walt,* from adapting it to new theories that are better suited for the post-Cold War environment, like offensive* and defensive realism.*

At the same time, neorealism has also influenced the emergence of a new approach, neoclassical realism,* which is now considered a distinct theoretical branch of international relations. This model combines two levels of analysis:

First, an emphasis on the structure of the international system and, second, classical realist ideas of human imperfection. Neoclassical realists include the American theorists Gideon Rose,* Fareed Zakaria,* and Richard Ned Lebow.*

In Current Scholarship

Theory remains part of the mainstream of the field of international relations. Current promoters of neorealism, like Mearsheimer, Walt, Robert Gilpin,* and Robert Jervis,* have all reinforced Waltz's focus on the international system to the exclusion of considering the role of the states themselves. They tend to avoid analysis of state-level factors (the leadership of individual countries, for example), assuming instead that all states are basically similar in their desire for security.

The main way neorealism has remained important has been through the addition of new objects of analysis, often at the domestic level. Jervis, for example, added psychological factors of communication to his evaluation of the roots of war. He believed miscommunication of ideas between states causes war in two ways: the "deterrence" model and the "spiral" model.[4]

Similarly, Mearsheimer offered a different version of neorealism in his 2001 book, *The Tragedy of Great Power Politics*, where he introduced the idea of offensive realism. According to offensive realist theory, states seek to maximize their power relative to one another, rather than to get "just enough" power to maintain security. For traditional neorealists,* states obtain "just enough" security by preserving a balance of power with their enemies. Mearsheimer, in contrast, argued that states never have "just enough" security, that great powers will always increase their security by getting as much power as they can, and that those powers will aggressively put down other states whenever possible.[5]

Although Waltz's traditional form of neorealism may no longer be a leading model for the study of today's international relations, his disciples have managed to adapt his model in such a way that it continues to be a prominent and influential school of thought.

NOTES

1   Chris Brown and Kirsten Ainley, *Understanding International Relations* (London: Palgrave McMillan, 2005). 33.

2   Ole Wæver, "The Rise and Fall of the Inter-Paradigm Debate," in *International Theory: Positivism and Beyond*, ed. Steve Smith, Ken Booth, and Marysia Zalewski (Cambridge: Cambridge University Press, 1996), 163.

3   See Alexander Wendt, "Anarchy is What States Make of It: the Social Construction of Power Politics," *International Organization* 46, no. 2 (1992): 391–425.

4   Robert Jervis, *Perception and Misperception in International Politics* (Princeton, NJ: Princeton University Press, 1976), 94. In this model, an aggressive state is appeased in the hope of eliciting better behavior, but the aggressive state only sees that it is capable of frightening its adversaries into concessions and, therefore, continues that behavior, leading to war. Conversely, in the "spiral" model, an aggressive state is punished in the hope of eliciting better behavior, but the aggressive state sees the punishment as aggression and perceives the need to defend itself more assertively, leading to war.

5   John Mearsheimer, "Structural Realism," in *International Relations Theories*, ed. Tim Dunne, Milja Kurki, and Steve Smith (Oxford: Oxford University Press, 2007), 72–73.

IMPACT AND INFLUENCE TODAY

KEY POINTS

- After the end of the Cold War,* Kenneth Waltz's followers updated his *Theory of International Politics*. The neorealist* scholar John Mearsheimer,* for example, wrote that the new situation was multipolar,* with competition and war more likely that before.

- After Waltz published his book, two new schools of thought, constructivism* and critical theory,* attacked it for assuming that relations between countries ran along somewhat mechanical and predictable, lines. For them, *Theory* failed to account for the influence of culture and the political choices that countries can make.

- The end of the Cold War has led to new schools of thought that—whether they argue, on the one hand, that countries tend toward competition or, on the other, toward cooperation—all allow for more human choice in international affairs that Waltz did.

Position

Kenneth Waltz's *Theory of International Politics* defined international relations theory toward the end of the Cold War. His main aim when writing the book was to create a scientifically-based model to explain war, balances of power,* alliances, and other common aspects of international affairs. In that, he was very successful.

The sudden end of the Cold War in 1991, however, revealed the limits of his theory. Even so, a number of Waltz's followers, particularly the American neorealist theorist John Mearsheimer, have adapted and

> 66 Contemporary realists remain committed to the goal
> of peace but find it difficult to accept that the postwar
> behavior of the great powers had belied their unduly
> pessimistic assumptions about the consequences of
> anarchy.* 99
>
> Richard Ned Lebow, "The Long Peace, the End of the Cold War, and the
> Failure of Realism"

modernized the model to better reflect the current international
setting. As a result, the text remains relevant to assessing international
affairs today.

Waltz's major contribution to his field was in shifting the type of
analysis from political philosophy to hard science through the
application of a positivist* method. He intended his theory to offer
laws that were enduring with repeatable predictions, somewhat like
laws of physics. Waltz advanced a number of beliefs about the
international system that were "natural" and "inevitable," like his belief
that global politics is shaped exclusively by its "great power" players.[1]
But in the aftermath of the Cold War, the international system clearly
shifted away from bipolarity* toward multipolarity,* as "secondary"
states and non-state actors began to influence international affairs.

Even before the collapse of the Soviet Union* in late 1991, for
example, Mearsheimer had predicted the emergence of a multipolar
international system in his 1990 article "Back to the Future."
Mearsheimer argued that an end to the Cold War would see the rise of
a new international system where power and influence would be
concentrated in the hands of three or more players, which would result
in more—rather than less—competition and war between countries.[2]

Interaction

Since the publication of *Theory*, Waltz's ideas have seen challenges from two new schools of thought: constructivism and critical theory.

Constructivists claim that major features of international relations are made by particular societies in their historical situation. In other words, those features are not simply the outcome of human nature.[3] In 1992, Alexander Wendt,* a leading constructivist, published an article that challenged Waltz's belief that the anarchy of the international system caused states to act selfishly and compete.[4] In short, Wendt's position was that states did not have fixed identities and interests— they could choose to see themselves as competitive or cooperative. This meant that the international system could be defined by cooperation if states chose to cooperate.

Critical theorists, like the German thinker Friedrich Kratochwil,* issued an even more basic criticism of neorealism's methodology. In an article from 1993, "The Embarrassment of Changes," Kratochwil argued that the "search for invariable [unchanging] laws of international politics has not only significantly reduced the set of interesting questions, it has also led to premature closure."[5] He claimed that neorealism tried to describe international affairs in such a mechanical way that it failed to consider the "social" aspect of how people and countries act.

The Continuing Debate
Today, the intensity of the debate around Waltz's text has relaxed somewhat, particularly compared to the early 1990s. One reason for that has been the emergence of new theories that view neorealism as a source of inspiration, among them offensive realism* and neoclassical realism.*

Perhaps Waltz's most well-known follower is John Mearsheimer, whose famous 2001 text, *The Tragedy of Great Power Politics,* adapted neorealism to better suit the state of international affairs at the time. In place of neorealism, Mearsheimer introduced the idea of offensive realism, which argued that states have sought to maximize their power relative to one another, rather than have "just enough" to feel secure.

This theory differed from neorealism in the sense that Mearsheimer believed states could never achieve total security. He thought that great powers—like the United States, Russia, and more recently China—will try to increase their security by maximizing their power and will aggressively put down smaller states when challenged.[6]

Similarly, in the early 1990s, a group of scholars developed a new mode of realist analysis by joining together key parts of neorealism with classical realism.* The resulting neoclassical realism,* according to the American international relations scholar Gideon Rose,* "explicitly incorporates both external [the international system] and internal [domestic] variables, updating and systemizing certain insights drawn from Classical Realist thought."[7] For example, Richard Ned Lebow,* a leading member of the school, challenged Waltz's claim that neorealism remained important after the Cold War and the break-up of the Soviet Union.

The problem, according to Lebow, was that Waltz continued to insist that the post-Cold War world continued to be bipolar,* a view at odds with those of other realists.[8] In response, neoclassical realists found inspiration from classical realist scholars, like Hans Morgenthau,* and sought to capture the "human" aspects in their analysis of international affairs, accounting for society and the roles played by world leaders.

Ultimately, neither offensive realists nor neoclassical realists are debating the central ideas put forward in *Theory,* but are instead using Waltz's text to develop new ways of analysis that are better suited for evaluating the post-Cold War international environment. Both of these theories stand in opposition to neoliberals,* like Joseph Nye* and Robert Keohane,* who maintain that cooperation—not competition—is the more common aim of countries today, and constructivists,* like Alexander Wendt, and critical theorists,* like Friedrich Kratochwil,* who have argued for a more open approach to theorizing that takes into account identity, interests, and process.

NOTES

1   Kenneth Waltz, *Theory of International Politics* (Reading: Addison Wesley, 1979), 73.

2   John Mearsheimer, "Back to the Future: Instability in Europe after the Cold War," *International Security* 15, no. 1 (1990): 5.

3   Patrick Thaddeus Jackson and Daniel H. Nexon, "Whence Causal Mechanisms? A Comment on Legro," *Dialogue IO* 1, no. 1 (2002): 81.

4   Alexander Wendt, "Anarchy is What States Make of It: The Social Construction of Power Politics," *International Organization* 46, no. 2 (1992): 417.

5   Friedrich Kratochwil, "The Embarrassment of Changes: Neorealism as the Science of Realpolitik without Politics," *Review of International Studies* 19, no. 1 (1993): 64.

6   John Mearsheimer, "Structural Realism," in *International Relations Theories*, ed. Tim Dunne, Milja Kurki, and Steve Smith (Oxford: Oxford University Press, 2007): 72–3.

7   Gideon Rose, "Neoclassical Realism and Theories of Foreign Policy," *World Politics* 51, no. 1 (1998): 146.

8   Richard Ned Lebow, "The Long Peace, the End of the Cold War, and the Failure of Realism," *International Organization* 48, no. 2 (1994): 254.

WHERE NEXT?

KEY POINTS

- Kenneth Waltz's approach in *Theory of International Politics* led him to argue that nuclear weapons are a stabilizing factor, making the price of war too terrible for countries to enter into armed conflict.

- Revived tensions between the West and Russia over Ukraine* have resulted in a renewed interest in neorealist* theory.

- By injecting a scientific, system-wide approach to international relations, Waltz's *Theory* has had a major impact on the discipline.

Potential

Kenneth Waltz's *Theory of International Politics* has had a lasting influence on the study of international relations and will continue to be a key text in the future. The book continues to be cited in major publications, including the *US Army War College Guide to National Security Policy and Strategy*,[1] and has also been a source of inspiration to top government officials, like Condoleezza Rice, a former US secretary of state.*[2] This suggests that future policymakers and scholars will view Waltz's text as a basic source for the study of international affairs.

The real-world uses of Waltz's *Theory* came through in his later work, where he sought to build upon this original theoretical foundation. For example, in his debate with Scott Sagan,* Waltz argued that nuclear weapons in the hands of all states would "make the cost of war seem frighteningly high and thus discourage states from starting any wars that might lead to the use of such weapons."[3]

> **❝** Miscalculation by some or all of the great powers is the source of danger in a multipolar world; overreaction by either or both of the great powers is the source of danger in a bipolar world. Bipolarity encourages the Soviet Union [or Russia] and United States to turn unwanted events into crises, while rendering most of them relatively inconsequential. Each can lose heavily in a war against the other; in power and wealth, both gain more by peaceful development of internal resources. **❞**
>
> Kenneth Waltz, *Theory of International Politics*

Therefore, states armed with conventional weapons were more likely to fight one another than nuclear-armed states. Waltz believed that two nuclear-armed states would not risk nuclear conflict because both parties would be completely destroyed in the event of a war, whereas two conventionally armed states would fight until one defeated the other.

In 2012, Waltz repeated his argument in an article for *Foreign Affairs*, "Why Iran Should Get the Bomb," suggesting that "power begs to be balanced" and that nuclear states become less likely to go to war.[4] This shows that Waltz's theory can still be applied to conflicts between countries, although not necessarily to great power competition.

Future Directions

Modern neorealists have attempted to update Waltz's theory by loosening some of its more rigid ideas. For example, the American neorealist thinker Stephen Walt,* who had introduced the concept of "balance of threat"* to the neorealist vocabulary in the mid-1980s, has argued that the classical realist* idea of a "balance of power"* did not accurately capture all the details of global politics today. Walt claimed that "the degree to which a state threatens others is a function of four factors: its aggregate power, geographic proximity, offensive capabilities, and offensive intentions." This, he said, was the strongest basis for analyzing international relations.

For example, how was the United States able to create a powerful coalition of allies to contain the Soviet Union* during the Cold War*? The reason, according to Walt, was that the Soviets "possessed significant aggregate power, was close to other key centers of world power, had large offensive capabilities, and at different times proclaimed openly revisionist aims."[5] In other words, the Soviet Union was a threat to everyone.

Interestingly, in the immediate post-Cold War environment, critics who felt neorealism was no longer useful to the analysis of international relations had lampooned the approach. But these critics failed to consider the possibility of a renewed competition between the United States and Russia, which became a reality in 2014 after Russia annexed the Crimean region of Ukraine and sparked a civil war and major international crisis. It was at this point that neorealism seemed to come back as a useful model.

In September 2014, the American neorealist scholar Mearsheimer published the article "Why The Ukraine Crisis is the West's Fault," which argued that Russia interpreted the expansion of Western influence, through the spread of the North Atlantic Treaty Organization (NATO)* and the European Union (EU)* into Eastern Europe, as a threat to its interests.

"In essence, the two sides have been operating with different playbooks: [Vladimir] Putin* and his compatriots have been thinking and acting according to realist* dictates, whereas their Western counterparts have been adhering to liberal ideas about international politics," Mearsheimer said. In other words, the Russians viewed the expansion of NATO and the EU as the creation of an anti-Russia order on its border, which made it feel threatened. Therefore, Mearsheimer concludes, "The United States and its allies unknowingly provoked a major crisis over Ukraine."[6] This analysis is an excellent example of the application of the neorealist approach to current affairs, signaling its potential to remain a relevant method of analysis in the future.

Summary

Kenneth Waltz's *Theory* deserves special attention as a major contribution to the theory of international relations during the Cold War. By using a more positivist* (that is, scientific) approach to the study of international affairs, Waltz established an entirely new school of thought, neorealism, which has been a major subject of debate ever since.

Contemporary international relations, observed the theorist of international politics Chris Brown,* "is fixated on *Theory of International Politics.* Not only was realism revitalized by this book, but also anti-Realists have felt obliged to respond to its arguments."[7] Indeed, Waltz was entirely successful at achieving the revolution in the study of international relations that he had aimed for, having radically changed the way that scholars understand what goes on when countries interact. He did so by, 1) illustrating what a scientific theory should look like; 2) identifying the problems in existing theories; 3) introducing a new, scientific model; and 4) finally applying this model to current issues. From this point onward, the entire field of international relations was transformed, as scholars were forced to adapt to this radically new approach.

At its root, what made Waltz's work so special at the time was its originality. Rather than continuing the common approach of looking at the specific traits of individual states and their leaders, he applied a system-wide and scientific method. In this way, he transformed an academic discipline that had been historically part of the humanities— one that was more similar to history or philosophy than to a social science like economics. *Theory* has been credited with completing the modernization of a discipline that was stuck in a classical realist* way of thinking. As such, it had an enormous impact on academics, and it will remain one of the most important texts in the history of international relations.

NOTES

1   John F. Troxell, "Military Power and The Use of Force," *US Army War College Guide to National Security Policy and Strategy*, ed. J. Boone Bartholomees Jr. (Carlisle, PA: US Army, 2006), 62.

2   Alec Russell, "US Foreign Policy Takes Neo-Realist Approach," *The Telegraph*, February 9, 2006, accessed December 6, 2013, http://www.telegraph.co.uk/news/worldnews/northamerica/usa/1510075/US-foreign-policy-takes-neo-realist-approach.html.

3   Kenneth Waltz, *The Spread of Nuclear Weapons: More May Be Better* (London: International Institute for Strategic Studies, 1981), 1.

4   Kenneth Waltz, "Why Iran Should Get the Bomb," *Foreign Affairs* 91, no. 4 (2012), accessed August 29, 2013, http://www.foreignaffairs.com/articles/137731/kenneth-n-waltz/why-iran-should-get-the-bomb.

5   *Yale Journal of International Affairs*, "Balancing Threat: The United States and The Middle East: An Interview with Stephen M. Walt," September 10, 2010, accessed January 15, 2015, http://yalejournal.org/wp-content/uploads/2010/09/105202walt.pdf.

6   John Mearsheimer, "Why The Ukraine Crisis is the West's Fault," *Foreign Affairs* 93, no. 5 (2014), accessed December 12, 2014, http://www.foreignaffairs.com/articles/141769/john-j-mearsheimer/why-the-ukraine-crisis-is-the-wests-fault.

7   Chris Brown and Kirsten Ainley, *Understanding International Relations* (London: Palgrave MacMillan, 2005), 40.

GLOSSARY

GLOSSARY OF TERMS

Absolute gain: a means by which international actors (countries or organizations) determine their interests, weighing out the total effects of a decision on themselves and acting accordingly.

Al-Qaeda: a militant Islamic fundamentalist group that was behind a terrorist attack against the United States on September 11, 2001.

Anarchy: a state of leaderlessness; sovereign states are in an anarchic world because there is no authority compelling them to act one way or another.

Balance of power: a balance of power refers to the conditions whereby the power of one state is balanced by the equivalent power of another state or group of states.

Balance of threat: a theory that holds that states use four criteria to evaluate the threat of another state: 1) aggregate strength, 2) geographic proximity, 3) offensive capabilities, and 4) offensive intentions.

Bipolar: a distribution of power in the international system; a bipolar system has power concentrated in two states, whereas a unipolar system has only one pole (also known as hegemony); a multipolar system has power concentrated among three or more states.

Bosnian War (1992–5): an armed conflict that took place in Bosnia and Herzegovina after the break-up of the state of Yugoslavia.

Classical realism: school of international relations theory that assumes state action is agent-driven (controlled by leaders, rather than structural imperative) and identifies the inherent imperfections of human nature as the source of conflict.

Cold War (1947–91): a period of tension between the United States and the Soviet Union and the nations aligned to them. While the two blocs never engaged in direct military conflict, they engaged in covert and proxy wars as well as espionage against one another.

Constructivism: a school of international relations that has gained prominence since the end of the Cold War. This school of thought believes that both historical and social factors, as opposed to human nature, determine international politics.

Copernican Revolution: a metaphor used to describe an overhaul of a discipline to replace "common sense" and traditional explanations with a radically new way to think about the discipline, one based on pure science. It refers to the observation of the Polish astronomer Nicolaus Copernicus in the fifteenth century that the earth revolved around the sun—not the sun around the earth.

Critical theory: a school of thought that originated in Frankfurt in the 1930s. It is concerned with the circumstances and assumptions that underpin ideas in social sciences and the humanities.

Defensive realism: a theoretical concept that argues that the anarchy of the international system forces states to become obsessed with security, which leads to security dilemmas whereby a state's drive for security can lead to conflict with its opponents.

Détente: a policy that the United States implemented between 1971 and 1980 to deal with the Soviet Union. The policy consisted of easing tensions through less provocative behavior and interaction via meetings and summits.

European Union: a family of institutions that govern the legal, economic, and political union of 28 European states.

Game theory: a branch of strategic studies that uses mathematical models to analyze potential strategies for responding to competitive— or zero-sum—situations, whereby one side wins and another loses. The models help predict the best possible approach to a particular situation and are often used in international relations to predict the actions of an opponent.

Great Debate: a debate that took place among theorists of the neoliberal,* neorealist,* critical theory,* and constructivist* schools of thought and that was largely documented in two academic journals, *International Organization* and *International Security*.

Hegemony: leadership or dominance, especially by one country or social group over others. When a state achieves dominance over all other states, they are considered a hegemon.

Hierarchy: a state of clear authority. States in a hierarchical world can be compelled by other, more powerful states or some non-state actor one way or another.

High politics: diplomatic-strategic issues relevant to the survival of the state.

Inductivism: a scientific method developed by the English philosopher Francis Bacon (1561–1626) that makes a "modest observation" based on a pattern of observed behavior in nature, which can be confirmed by the collection of further data and eventually developed into a theory or law.

Islamic State of Iraq and Syria/the Levant (ISIS or ISIL): an Islamist militant group that seized control of a large amount of territory in both Iraq and Syria in 2014.

Korean War (1950–3): a Cold War conflict that began when North Korea invaded South Korea in 1950, leading to a United Nations intervention that lasted until a ceasefire was declared in 1953. The war technically continues to this day.

League of Nations (1920–46): an international organization founded in the aftermath of World War I and considered to be the precursor to the modern United Nations.

Liberalism (international relations): a school of international relations theory that suggests that states can, and ultimately will, achieve peace and mutual cooperation.

Low politics: cultural-economic issues relevant to the welfare of the state.

Multipolar: a distribution of power within the international system whereby power is balanced between more than two nations.

Neoclassical realism: a combination of neorealism* and classical realism.* Its supporters hold that state action can be explained with reference to both structural factors (such as the distribution of capabilities between states) and agent-driven factors (such as the ambitions of given leaders).

Neocolonialism: a perspective that assumes that international capitalism drives states to acquire empires, either by direct means or indirect military control.

Neoliberal institutionalism: see neoliberalism.

Neoliberalism: school of international relations theory that holds that cooperation among countries is possible and likely, especially through international institutions, because states prefer to maximize their absolute gains rather than their relative gains over one another.

Neorealism/structural realism: a school of international relations theory that assumes structural constraints (anarchy and the distribution of world power), rather than human agency, will determine an actor's behavior.

North Atlantic Treaty Organization (NATO): a collective defense organization composed of 28 states. It is generally considered to be engaged in the promotion of American, or Western, interests abroad.

Offensive realism: a theory of international relations first put forward by John J. Mearsheimer, arguing that aggressive behavior between states at an international level is a result of the lack of a central international authority.

Polarity: a distribution of power within the international system. A bipolar system has power concentrated in two states, whereas a unipolar system has only one pole (also known as hegemony) and a multipolar system has power concentrated among three or more states.

Positivism: a perspective in the philosophy of science. It holds that people obtain information through their sensory experience (what is seen and heard in the real world). Laws are derived from these observations and tested through experimentation.

Post-positivism: a response to positivism that holds that the background or values of the researcher can affect what he or she observes.

Quantitative analysis: the study of a situation or event using complex mathematical and statistical modeling.

Realism: a school of international relations theory that assumes, 1) states are the primary actors, 2) states all share the goal of survival, and 3) states provide for their own security.

Reductionism: a philosophical perspective that holds that a person can understand a system by examining its individual parts rather than as a working whole.

Relative gain: a means by which international actors determine their interests with respect to power balances while disregarding other key factors, such as economics.

Soviet Union, or USSR: a kind of "super state" that existed from 1922 to 1991, centered primarily on Russia and its neighbors in Eastern Europe and the northern half of Asia. It was the communist pole of the Cold War, with the United States as its main "rival."

Superpower: a very powerful and influential nation, often used to refer to the United States and the Soviet Union during the Cold War, when both states were the most powerful nations in the world.

Unipolar: an international situation where one nation dominates the rest (also known as hegemony).

Ukraine: a nation in which demonstrations in 2004 against its president, Viktor Yanukovych, aligned to Russia and perceived to be corrupt, finished in the re-election of Viktor Yushchenko as president. In controversial circumstances, Russia sponsored forces of ethnic Russians in the Crimean region to agitate for it to be incorporated into the Russian state. The crisis is ongoing.

United Nations: an intergovernmental organization representing nearly every state in the world. It is the main organization administering international health, development, security, and similar programs.

Vietnam War (1955–75): a Cold War conflict between the United States and the communist forces of North Vietnam. In 1973, the US signed a peace treaty and withdrew its forces from South Vietnam, which collapsed two years later.

World War I (1914–18): a military conflict between the Allied forces, led by France, Italy, Russia, the United Kingdom, and (after 1917) the United States, and the Central powers, led by Austria-Hungary, Bulgaria, Germany, and the Ottoman Empire. The war left 16 million people dead.

World War II (1939–45): a global conflict fought between the Axis Powers (Germany, Italy, and Japan) and the victorious Allied Powers (United Kingdom and its commonwealth, the former Soviet Union, and the United States).

Yugoslav Wars (1991–2001): a series of wars fought in south-eastern Europe's Balkan peninsula between the successor states to the former Yugoslavia, including Serbia and Montenegro, Bosnia and Herzegovina, Kosovo, Croatia, and Slovenia.

Zero-sum: a concept used in international relations to describe a situation whereby a victory for one side of a conflict is viewed as a loss for the other. For example, the United States viewed the Soviet Union's launching of Sputnik in 1957 as a loss.

PEOPLE MENTIONED IN THE TEXT

Mortimer Adler (1902–2001) was an American philosopher who wrote primarily on ethical topics. His work consisted of a wide range of ethical investigations into subjects from religion to the idea of human perfectibility to politics. He wrote *How to Think About War and Peace* in 1944.

Richard Ashley is a British international relations theorist in the critical theory school of thought.

Chris Brown is a prominent professor of international political theory at the London School of Economics.

Zbigniew Brzezinski (b. 1928) is a Polish-born American political scientist, statesman, and diplomat. He played a prominent role during the Jimmy Carter administration, serving as national security advisor in 1977–81.

Nicolaus Copernicus (1473–1543) was a Renaissance astronomer who showed that the sun and not the earth was at the center of the known universe.

Émile Durkheim (1858–1917) was a French social theorist. He is considered to be one of the founding fathers of the social sciences. Durkheim was concerned with imparting "hard" scientific rigor to the social sciences and the study of society as a system, rather than with individuals.

William T. R. Fox (1912–88), was an influential professor of foreign policy and an international relations theoretician from the US. In

1944, he coined the term "superpower."

Robert Gilpin (b. 1930) is an American professor of political economy at Princeton University. He is the author of a number of prominent works including *The Political Economy of International Relations*. Notably, he imported a key idea of neorealism into the field of political economy.

Robert Jervis (b. 1940) is an American professor of international affairs at Columbia University. He is associated with the neorealist school. Jervis is prominent for applying psychology to international conflict and positing how miscommunication between states can spiral into war.

Robert Keohane (b. 1941) is an American political science professor at Princeton. He is associated with neoliberal institutionalism, and he co-wrote his first book on the topic, *Power and Interdependence*, with Joseph Nye.

Henry Kissinger (b. 1923) is a German-born American political scientist, statesman, and diplomat. He played a prominent role during the administrations of US presidents Richard Nixon and Gerald Ford, first as national security advisor in 1969–73 and then as secretary of state in 1973–7.

Friedrich Kratochwil (b. 1944) is a German international relations scholar who has worked in both Europe and the United States. His 1989 book, *Rules, Norms, and Decisions*, is credited with introducing constructivism to the discipline.

Richard Ned Lebow is an American political scientist in the constructivist and neoclassical realist school of thought.

John Mearsheimer (b. 1947) is an American international relations professor and neorealist at the University of Chicago. He is the pioneer of "offensive realism," a contemporary reformulation of neorealism.

Hans Morgenthau (1904–80) was a German political theorist who worked primarily in America. He has been described as the most prominent of the classical realists.

Richard Nixon (1913–94) was the 37th president of the United States from 1969 to 1974. After securing a second term in office in 1972, he was forced to resign due to his involvement in the Watergate scandal.

Joseph Nye (b. 1937) is an American political science professor at Harvard University. He co-wrote *Power and Interdependence* with Robert Keohane, effectively founding neoliberal institutionalism.

Vladimir Putin (b. 1952) is a former Russian intelligence officer and statesman. He was president of the Russian Federation in 2000–8, prime minister in 2008–12, and has been president since 2012.

Condoleezza Rice (b. 1964) is a political scientist and diplomat. She played a prominent role in the administration of US President George W. Bush, first as national security advisor (2001–05) and then as secretary of state (2005–9).

Gideon Rose is an American professor and policy advisor in international relations. The editor of *Foreign Affairs* magazine from 2010, he teaches at Columbia University.

Scott Sagan (b. 1955) is an American professor of international relations at Stanford University. He is known for his research on nuclear weapons.

Thucydides (460–395 B.C.E.**)** was an ancient Athenian historian, politician, writer, and general. He is often thought of as the first political theorist.

Ole Wæver (b. 1960) is a Danish professor of international relations, working primarily in Denmark and London and specializing in the theory of theory.

Stephen Walt (b. 1958) is an American international relations professor and neorealist. He co-wrote The *Israel Lobby and US Foreign Policy* with fellow neorealist John Mearsheimer. He expanded the concept of the "balance of power" to take state identities into account, calling it the "balance of threat."

Alexander Wendt (b. 1958) is a German political theorist and one of a core group of constructivist scholars in the field of international relations.

Woodrow Wilson (1856–1924) was the 28th President of the United States. He is notable for presiding over the US during World War I (1914–18) and for helping construct an international order in the aftermath.

Fareed Zakaria (b. 1964) is an Indian American journalist, author, and neorealist scholar. He has been managing editor of *Foreign Affairs* and *Time*, and he notably authored *The Post-American World*.

WORKS CITED

WORKS CITED

Adler, Mortimer. *How to Think About War and Peace*. New York: Simon and Schuster, 1944.

Ashley, Richard. "The Poverty of Neorealism." *Neorealism and Its Critics*, edited by Robert Keohane, 255–300. New York: Columbia University Press, 1986.

Booth, Ken. "The Darwin of International Relations." Foreign Policy. Accessed December 6, 2013. http://www.foreignpolicy.com/articles/2013/05/15/requiem_for_a_realist_kenneth_waltz?page=0,4.

Brown, Chris, and Kirsten Ainley. *Understanding International Relations*. London: Palgrave Macmillan, 2005.

Halliday, Fred, and Justin Rosenberg. "Interview with Ken Waltz." *Review of International Studies* 24, no. 3 (1998): 371–86.

Jervis, Robert. *Perception and Misperception in International Politics*. Princeton, NJ: Princeton University Press, 1976.

Kratochwil, Friedrich, "The Embarrassment of Changes: Neorealism as the Science of Realpolitik without Politics." *Review of International Studies* 19, no. 1 (1993): 63–80.

Kriesler, Harry. Theory and International Politics: Conversation with Kenneth Waltz. Accessed August 12, 2013. http://globetrotter.berkeley.edu/people3/Waltz/.

Lebow, Richard Ned. "Classical Realism." In *International Relations Theories*, edited by Tim Dunne, Milja Kurki, and Steve Smith, 52–69. Oxford: Oxford University Press, 2007.

Legro Jeffrey, and Andrew Moravcsik. "Is Anybody Still a Realist?" *International Security* 24, no. 2 (1999): 5–55.

Linklater, Andrew. "The Achievements of Critical Theory." In *International Theory: Positivism and Beyond*, edited by Steve Smith, Ken Booth, and Marysia Zalewski. Cambridge: Cambridge University Press, 1996.

Mearsheimer, John, "Back to the Future: Instability in Europe after the Cold War," *International Security* 15, no.1 (1990): 5–56.

"Structural Realism." In *International Relations Theories,* edited by Tim Dunne, Milja Kurki, and Steve Smith, 72–86. Oxford: Oxford University Press, 2007.

"Why The Ukraine Crisis is the West's Fault," Foreign Affairs 93, no. 5 (2014). Accessed December 12, 2014. http://www.foreignaffairs.com/articles/141769/john-j-mearsheimer/why-the-ukraine-crisis-is-the-wests-fault.

Milner, Helen. "Rationalizing Politics: The Emerging Synthesis of International, American, and Comparative Politics." *International Organization* 52, no. 4 (1998): 759–86.

Morgenthau, Hans. *Politics Among Nations.* New York: McGraw Hill, 1979.

Nye, Joseph. "Neorealism and Neoliberalism." *World Politics* 40, no. 2 (1988): 235–51.

Rose, Gideon. "Neoclassical Realism and Theories of Foreign Policy," *World Politics* 51, no. 1 (1998): 144–72.

Schouten, Peer. "Theory Talk #33, Stephen Walt." Theory Talks. Accessed November 1, 2013. http:/www.theory-talks.org/2011/06/theory-talk-33.html.

"Theory Talk #40, Kenneth Waltz." Theory Talks. Accessed August 14, 2013. http:/www.theory-talks.org/2011/06/theory-talk-40.html.

 Singer, David J. "The Level of Analysis Problem in International Relations." *World Politics* 14, no. 1 (1961): 77–91.

Troxell, John F. "Military Power and The Use of Force." In *US Army War College Guide to National Security Policy and Strategy*, edited by J. Boone Bartholomees Jr. Carlisle, PA: US Army, 2006.

Waever, Ole. "Waltz's Theory of Theory." *International Politics* 23, no. 2 (2009): 201–22.

Walt, Stephen. "Alliance Formation and the Balance of World Power." *International Security* 9, no. 4 (1985): 3–43.

Waltz, Kenneth. *Man, the State, and War: A Theoretical Analysis.* New York: Columbia University Press, 1959.

Theory of International Politics: A Theoretical Analysis. Reading: Addison Wesley, 1979.

The Spread of Nuclear Weapons: More May Be Better. London: International Institute for Strategic Studies, 1981.

"A Response to My Critics." In *Neorealism and Its Critics*, edited by Robert Keohane, 322–45. New York: Columbia University Press, 1986.

"Realist Thought and Neorealist Theory." *Journal of International Affairs* 44, no. 1 (1990): 21–37.

"The Emerging Structure of International Politics." *International Security* 18, no. 2 (1993): 44–79.

"Structural Realism After the Cold War." *International Security* 25, no. 1 (2000): 5–41.

"Why Iran Should Get the Bomb." Foreign Affairs. Accessed August 29, 2013. http://www.foreignaffairs.com/articles/137731/kenneth-n-waltz/why-iran-should-get-the-bomb.

Wendt, Alexander. "Anarchy is What States Make of It: The Social Construction of International Politics." *International Organization* 46, no. 2 (1992): 391–425.

Williams, Michael. "Waltz, Realism, and Democracy." *International Relations* 23, no. 3 (2009): 328–40.

THE MACAT LIBRARY
BY DISCIPLINE

AFRICANA STUDIES

Chinua Achebe's *An Image of Africa: Racism in Conrad's Heart of Darkness*
W. E. B. Du Bois's *The Souls of Black Folk*
Zora Neale Huston's *Characteristics of Negro Expression*
Martin Luther King Jr's *Why We Can't Wait*
Toni Morrison's *Playing in the Dark: Whiteness in the American Literary Imagination*

ANTHROPOLOGY

Arjun Appadurai's *Modernity at Large: Cultural Dimensions of Globalisation*
Philippe Ariès's *Centuries of Childhood*
Franz Boas's *Race, Language and Culture*
Kim Chan & Renée Mauborgne's *Blue Ocean Strategy*
Jared Diamond's *Guns, Germs & Steel: the Fate of Human Societies*
Jared Diamond's *Collapse: How Societies Choose to Fail or Survive*
E. E. Evans-Pritchard's *Witchcraft, Oracles and Magic Among the Azande*
James Ferguson's *The Anti-Politics Machine*
Clifford Geertz's *The Interpretation of Cultures*
David Graeber's *Debt: the First 5000 Years*
Karen Ho's *Liquidated: An Ethnography of Wall Street*
Geert Hofstede's *Culture's Consequences: Comparing Values, Behaviors, Institutes and Organizations across Nations*
Claude Lévi-Strauss's *Structural Anthropology*
Jay Macleod's *Ain't No Makin' It: Aspirations and Attainment in a Low-Income Neighborhood*
Saba Mahmood's *The Politics of Piety: The Islamic Revival and the Feminist Subjec*t
Marcel Mauss's *The Gift*

BUSINESS

Jean Lave & Etienne Wenger's *Situated Learning*
Theodore Levitt's *Marketing Myopia*
Burton G. Malkiel's *A Random Walk Down Wall Street*
Douglas McGregor's *The Human Side of Enterprise*
Michael Porter's *Competitive Strategy: Creating and Sustaining Superior Performance*
John Kotter's *Leading Change*
C. K. Prahalad & Gary Hamel's *The Core Competence of the Corporation*

CRIMINOLOGY

Michelle Alexander's *The New Jim Crow: Mass Incarceration in the Age of Colorblindness*
Michael R. Gottfredson & Travis Hirschi's *A General Theory of Crime*
Richard Herrnstein & Charles A. Murray's *The Bell Curve: Intelligence and Class Structure in American Life*
Elizabeth Loftus's *Eyewitness Testimony*
Jay Macleod's *Ain't No Makin' It: Aspirations and Attainment in a Low-Income Neighborhood*
Philip Zimbardo's *The Lucifer Effect*

ECONOMICS

Janet Abu-Lughod's *Before European Hegemony*
Ha-Joon Chang's *Kicking Away the Ladder*
David Brion Davis's *The Problem of Slavery in the Age of Revolution*
Milton Friedman's *The Role of Monetary Policy*
Milton Friedman's *Capitalism and Freedom*
David Graeber's *Debt: the First 5000 Years*
Friedrich Hayek's *The Road to Serfdom*
Karen Ho's *Liquidated: An Ethnography of Wall Street*

The Macat Library By Discipline

John Maynard Keynes's *The General Theory of Employment, Interest and Money*
Charles P. Kindleberger's *Manias, Panics and Crashes*
Robert Lucas's *Why Doesn't Capital Flow from Rich to Poor Countries?*
Burton G. Malkiel's *A Random Walk Down Wall Street*
Thomas Robert Malthus's *An Essay on the Principle of Population*
Karl Marx's *Capital*
Thomas Piketty's *Capital in the Twenty-First Century*
Amartya Sen's *Development as Freedom*
Adam Smith's *The Wealth of Nations*
Nassim Nicholas Taleb's *The Black Swan: The Impact of the Highly Improbable*
Amos Tversky's & Daniel Kahneman's *Judgment under Uncertainty: Heuristics and Biases*
Mahbub Ul Haq's *Reflections on Human Development*
Max Weber's *The Protestant Ethic and the Spirit of Capitalism*

FEMINISM AND GENDER STUDIES

Judith Butler's *Gender Trouble*
Simone De Beauvoir's *The Second Sex*
Michel Foucault's *History of Sexuality*
Betty Friedan's *The Feminine Mystique*
Saba Mahmood's *The Politics of Piety: The Islamic Revival and the Feminist Subject*
Joan Wallach Scott's *Gender and the Politics of History*
Mary Wollstonecraft's *A Vindication of the Rights of Woman*
Virginia Woolf's *A Room of One's Own*

GEOGRAPHY

The Brundtland Report's *Our Common Future*
Rachel Carson's *Silent Spring*
Charles Darwin's *On the Origin of Species*
James Ferguson's *The Anti-Politics Machine*
Jane Jacobs's *The Death and Life of Great American Cities*
James Lovelock's *Gaia: A New Look at Life on Earth*
Amartya Sen's *Development as Freedom*
Mathis Wackernagel & William Rees's *Our Ecological Footprint*

HISTORY

Janet Abu-Lughod's *Before European Hegemony*
Benedict Anderson's *Imagined Communities*
Bernard Bailyn's *The Ideological Origins of the American Revolution*
Hanna Batatu's *The Old Social Classes And The Revolutionary Movements Of Iraq*
Christopher Browning's *Ordinary Men: Reserve Police Batallion 101 and the Final Solution in Poland*
Edmund Burke's *Reflections on the Revolution in France*
William Cronon's *Nature's Metropolis: Chicago And The Great West*
Alfred W. Crosby's *The Columbian Exchange*
Hamid Dabashi's *Iran: A People Interrupted*
David Brion Davis's *The Problem of Slavery in the Age of Revolution*
Nathalie Zemon Davis's *The Return of Martin Guerre*
Jared Diamond's *Guns, Germs & Steel: the Fate of Human Societies*
Frank Dikotter's *Mao's Great Famine*
John W Dower's *War Without Mercy: Race And Power In The Pacific War*
W. E. B. Du Bois's *The Souls of Black Folk*
Richard J. Evans's *In Defence of History*
Lucien Febvre's *The Problem of Unbelief in the 16th Century*
Sheila Fitzpatrick's *Everyday Stalinism*

Eric Foner's *Reconstruction: America's Unfinished Revolution, 1863-1877*
Michel Foucault's *Discipline and Punish*
Michel Foucault's *History of Sexuality*
Francis Fukuyama's *The End of History and the Last Man*
John Lewis Gaddis's *We Now Know: Rethinking Cold War History*
Ernest Gellner's *Nations and Nationalism*
Eugene Genovese's *Roll, Jordan, Roll: The World the Slaves Made*
Carlo Ginzburg's *The Night Battles*
Daniel Goldhagen's *Hitler's Willing Executioners*
Jack Goldstone's *Revolution and Rebellion in the Early Modern World*
Antonio Gramsci's *The Prison Notebooks*
Alexander Hamilton, John Jay & James Madison's *The Federalist Papers*
Christopher Hill's *The World Turned Upside Down*
Carole Hillenbrand's *The Crusades: Islamic Perspectives*
Thomas Hobbes's *Leviathan*
Eric Hobsbawm's *The Age Of Revolution*
John A. Hobson's *Imperialism: A Study*
Albert Hourani's *History of the Arab Peoples*
Samuel P. Huntington's *The Clash of Civilizations and the Remaking of World Order*
C. L. R. James's *The Black Jacobins*
Tony Judt's *Postwar: A History of Europe Since 1945*
Ernst Kantorowicz's *The King's Two Bodies: A Study in Medieval Political Theology*
Paul Kennedy's *The Rise and Fall of the Great Powers*
Ian Kershaw's *The "Hitler Myth": Image and Reality in the Third Reich*
John Maynard Keynes's *The General Theory of Employment, Interest and Money*
Charles P. Kindleberger's *Manias, Panics and Crashes*
Martin Luther King Jr's *Why We Can't Wait*
Henry Kissinger's *World Order: Reflections on the Character of Nations and the Course of History*
Thomas Kuhn's *The Structure of Scientific Revolutions*
Georges Lefebvre's *The Coming of the French Revolution*
John Locke's *Two Treatises of Government*
Niccolò Machiavelli's *The Prince*
Thomas Robert Malthus's *An Essay on the Principle of Population*
Mahmood Mamdani's *Citizen and Subject: Contemporary Africa And The Legacy Of Late Colonialism*
Karl Marx's *Capital*
Stanley Milgram's *Obedience to Authority*
John Stuart Mill's *On Liberty*
Thomas Paine's *Common Sense*
Thomas Paine's *Rights of Man*
Geoffrey Parker's *Global Crisis: War, Climate Change and Catastrophe in the Seventeenth Century*
Jonathan Riley-Smith's *The First Crusade and the Idea of Crusading*
Jean-Jacques Rousseau's *The Social Contract*
Joan Wallach Scott's *Gender and the Politics of History*
Theda Skocpol's *States and Social Revolutions*
Adam Smith's *The Wealth of Nations*
Timothy Snyder's *Bloodlands: Europe Between Hitler and Stalin*
Sun Tzu's *The Art of War*
Keith Thomas's *Religion and the Decline of Magic*
Thucydides's *The History of the Peloponnesian War*
Frederick Jackson Turner's *The Significance of the Frontier in American History*
Odd Arne Westad's *The Global Cold War: Third World Interventions And The Making Of Our Times*

The Macat Library By Discipline

LITERATURE

Chinua Achebe's *An Image of Africa: Racism in Conrad's Heart of Darkness*
Roland Barthes's *Mythologies*
Homi K. Bhabha's *The Location of Culture*
Judith Butler's *Gender Trouble*
Simone De Beauvoir's *The Second Sex*
Ferdinand De Saussure's *Course in General Linguistics*
T. S. Eliot's *The Sacred Wood: Essays on Poetry and Criticism*
Zora Neale Huston's *Characteristics of Negro Expression*
Toni Morrison's *Playing in the Dark: Whiteness in the American Literary Imagination*
Edward Said's *Orientalism*
Gayatri Chakravorty Spivak's *Can the Subaltern Speak?*
Mary Wollstonecraft's *A Vindication of the Rights of Women*
Virginia Woolf's *A Room of One's Own*

PHILOSOPHY

Elizabeth Anscombe's *Modern Moral Philosophy*
Hannah Arendt's *The Human Condition*
Aristotle's *Metaphysics*
Aristotle's *Nicomachean Ethics*
Edmund Gettier's *Is Justified True Belief Knowledge?*
Georg Wilhelm Friedrich Hegel's *Phenomenology of Spirit*
David Hume's *Dialogues Concerning Natural Religion*
David Hume's *The Enquiry for Human Understanding*
Immanuel Kant's *Religion within the Boundaries of Mere Reason*
Immanuel Kant's *Critique of Pure Reason*
Søren Kierkegaard's *The Sickness Unto Death*
Søren Kierkegaard's *Fear and Trembling*
C. S. Lewis's *The Abolition of Man*
Alasdair MacIntyre's *After Virtue*
Marcus Aurelius's *Meditations*
Friedrich Nietzsche's *On the Genealogy of Morality*
Friedrich Nietzsche's *Beyond Good and Evil*
Plato's *Republic*
Plato's *Symposium*
Jean-Jacques Rousseau's *The Social Contract*
Gilbert Ryle's *The Concept of Mind*
Baruch Spinoza's *Ethics*
Sun Tzu's *The Art of War*
Ludwig Wittgenstein's *Philosophical Investigations*

POLITICS

Benedict Anderson's *Imagined Communities*
Aristotle's *Politics*
Bernard Bailyn's *The Ideological Origins of the American Revolution*
Edmund Burke's *Reflections on the Revolution in France*
John C. Calhoun's *A Disquisition on Government*
Ha-Joon Chang's *Kicking Away the Ladder*
Hamid Dabashi's *Iran: A People Interrupted*
Hamid Dabashi's *Theology of Discontent: The Ideological Foundation of the Islamic Revolution in Iran*
Robert Dahl's *Democracy and its Critics*
Robert Dahl's *Who Governs?*
David Brion Davis's *The Problem of Slavery in the Age of Revolution*

Alexis De Tocqueville's *Democracy in America*
James Ferguson's *The Anti-Politics Machine*
Frank Dikotter's *Mao's Great Famine*
Sheila Fitzpatrick's *Everyday Stalinism*
Eric Foner's *Reconstruction: America's Unfinished Revolution, 1863-1877*
Milton Friedman's *Capitalism and Freedom*
Francis Fukuyama's *The End of History and the Last Man*
John Lewis Gaddis's *We Now Know: Rethinking Cold War History*
Ernest Gellner's *Nations and Nationalism*
David Graeber's *Debt: the First 5000 Years*
Antonio Gramsci's *The Prison Notebooks*
Alexander Hamilton, John Jay & James Madison's *The Federalist Papers*
Friedrich Hayek's *The Road to Serfdom*
Christopher Hill's *The World Turned Upside Down*
Thomas Hobbes's *Leviathan*
John A. Hobson's *Imperialism: A Study*
Samuel P. Huntington's *The Clash of Civilizations and the Remaking of World Order*
Tony Judt's *Postwar: A History of Europe Since 1945*
David C. Kang's *China Rising: Peace, Power and Order in East Asia*
Paul Kennedy's *The Rise and Fall of Great Powers*
Robert Keohane's *After Hegemony*
Martin Luther King Jr.'s *Why We Can't Wait*
Henry Kissinger's *World Order: Reflections on the Character of Nations and the Course of History*
John Locke's *Two Treatises of Government*
Niccolò Machiavelli's *The Prince*
Thomas Robert Malthus's *An Essay on the Principle of Population*
Mahmood Mamdani's *Citizen and Subject: Contemporary Africa And The Legacy Of Late Colonialism*
Karl Marx's *Capital*
John Stuart Mill's *On Liberty*
John Stuart Mill's *Utilitarianism*
Hans Morgenthau's *Politics Among Nations*
Thomas Paine's *Common Sense*
Thomas Paine's *Rights of Man*
Thomas Piketty's *Capital in the Twenty-First Century*
Robert D. Putman's *Bowling Alone*
John Rawls's *Theory of Justice*
Jean-Jacques Rousseau's *The Social Contract*
Theda Skocpol's *States and Social Revolutions*
Adam Smith's *The Wealth of Nations*
Sun Tzu's *The Art of War*
Henry David Thoreau's *Civil Disobedience*
Thucydides's *The History of the Peloponnesian War*
Kenneth Waltz's *Theory of International Politics*
Max Weber's *Politics as a Vocation*
Odd Arne Westad's *The Global Cold War: Third World Interventions And The Making Of Our Times*

POSTCOLONIAL STUDIES

Roland Barthes's *Mythologies*
Frantz Fanon's *Black Skin, White Masks*
Homi K. Bhabha's *The Location of Culture*
Gustavo Gutiérrez's *A Theology of Liberation*
Edward Said's *Orientalism*
Gayatri Chakravorty Spivak's *Can the Subaltern Speak?*

The Macat Library By Discipline

PSYCHOLOGY

Gordon Allport's *The Nature of Prejudice*
Alan Baddeley & Graham Hitch's *Aggression: A Social Learning Analysis*
Albert Bandura's *Aggression: A Social Learning Analysis*
Leon Festinger's *A Theory of Cognitive Dissonance*
Sigmund Freud's *The Interpretation of Dreams*
Betty Friedan's *The Feminine Mystique*
Michael R. Gottfredson & Travis Hirschi's *A General Theory of Crime*
Eric Hoffer's *The True Believer: Thoughts on the Nature of Mass Movements*
William James's *Principles of Psychology*
Elizabeth Loftus's *Eyewitness Testimony*
A. H. Maslow's *A Theory of Human Motivation*
Stanley Milgram's *Obedience to Authority*
Steven Pinker's *The Better Angels of Our Nature*
Oliver Sacks's *The Man Who Mistook His Wife For a Hat*
Richard Thaler & Cass Sunstein's *Nudge: Improving Decisions About Health, Wealth and Happiness*
Amos Tversky's *Judgment under Uncertainty: Heuristics and Biases*
Philip Zimbardo's *The Lucifer Effect*

SCIENCE

Rachel Carson's *Silent Spring*
William Cronon's *Nature's Metropolis: Chicago And The Great West*
Alfred W. Crosby's *The Columbian Exchange*
Charles Darwin's *On the Origin of Species*
Richard Dawkin's *The Selfish Gene*
Thomas Kuhn's *The Structure of Scientific Revolutions*
Geoffrey Parker's *Global Crisis: War, Climate Change and Catastrophe in the Seventeenth Century*
Mathis Wackernagel & William Rees's *Our Ecological Footprint*

SOCIOLOGY

Michelle Alexander's *The New Jim Crow: Mass Incarceration in the Age of Colorblindness*
Gordon Allport's *The Nature of Prejudice*
Albert Bandura's *Aggression: A Social Learning Analysis*
Hanna Batatu's *The Old Social Classes And The Revolutionary Movements Of Iraq*
Ha-Joon Chang's *Kicking Away the Ladder*
W. E. B. Du Bois's *The Souls of Black Folk*
Émile Durkheim's *On Suicide*
Frantz Fanon's *Black Skin, White Masks*
Frantz Fanon's *The Wretched of the Earth*
Eric Foner's *Reconstruction: America's Unfinished Revolution, 1863-1877*
Eugene Genovese's *Roll, Jordan, Roll: The World the Slaves Made*
Jack Goldstone's *Revolution and Rebellion in the Early Modern World*
Antonio Gramsci's *The Prison Notebooks*
Richard Herrnstein & Charles A Murray's *The Bell Curve: Intelligence and Class Structure in American Life*
Eric Hoffer's *The True Believer: Thoughts on the Nature of Mass Movements*
Jane Jacobs's *The Death and Life of Great American Cities*
Robert Lucas's *Why Doesn't Capital Flow from Rich to Poor Countries?*
Jay Macleod's *Ain't No Makin' It: Aspirations and Attainment in a Low Income Neighborhood*
Elaine May's *Homeward Bound: American Families in the Cold War Era*
Douglas McGregor's *The Human Side of Enterprise*
C. Wright Mills's *The Sociological Imagination*

Thomas Piketty's *Capital in the Twenty-First Century*
Robert D. Putman's *Bowling Alone*
David Riesman's *The Lonely Crowd: A Study of the Changing American Character*
Edward Said's *Orientalism*
Joan Wallach Scott's *Gender and the Politics of History*
Theda Skocpol's *States and Social Revolutions*
Max Weber's *The Protestant Ethic and the Spirit of Capitalism*

THEOLOGY

Augustine's *Confessions*
Benedict's *Rule of St Benedict*
Gustavo Gutiérrez's *A Theology of Liberation*
Carole Hillenbrand's *The Crusades: Islamic Perspectives*
David Hume's *Dialogues Concerning Natural Religion*
Immanuel Kant's *Religion within the Boundaries of Mere Reason*
Ernst Kantorowicz's *The King's Two Bodies: A Study in Medieval Political Theology*
Søren Kierkegaard's *The Sickness Unto Death*
C. S. Lewis's *The Abolition of Man*
Saba Mahmood's *The Politics of Piety: The Islamic Revival and the Feminist Subjec*t
Baruch Spinoza's *Ethics*
Keith Thomas's *Religion and the Decline of Magic*

COMING SOON

Chris Argyris's *The Individual and the Organisation*
Seyla Benhabib's *The Rights of Others*
Walter Benjamin's *The Work Of Art in the Age of Mechanical Reproduction*
John Berger's *Ways of Seeing*
Pierre Bourdieu's *Outline of a Theory of Practice*
Mary Douglas's *Purity and Danger*
Roland Dworkin's *Taking Rights Seriously*
James G. March's *Exploration and Exploitation in Organisational Learning*
Ikujiro Nonaka's *A Dynamic Theory of Organizational Knowledge Creation*
Griselda Pollock's *Vision and Difference*
Amartya Sen's *Inequality Re-Examined*
Susan Sontag's *On Photography*
Yasser Tabbaa's *The Transformation of Islamic Art*
Ludwig von Mises's *Theory of Money and Credit*

Macat Disciplines

Access the greatest ideas and thinkers across entire disciplines, including

AFRICANA STUDIES

Chinua Achebe's *An Image of Africa: Racism in Conrad's Heart of Darkness*

W. E. B. Du Bois's *The Souls of Black Folk*

Zora Neale Hurston's *Characteristics of Negro Expression*

Martin Luther King Jr.'s *Why We Can't Wait*

Toni Morrison's *Playing in the Dark: Whiteness in the American Literary Imagination*

Macat analyses are available from all good bookshops and libraries.

Access hundreds of analyses through one, multimedia tool.
Join free for one month **library.macat.com**

Macat Disciplines

*Access the greatest ideas and thinkers
across entire disciplines, including*

FEMINISM, GENDER AND QUEER STUDIES

Simone De Beauvoir's
The Second Sex

Michel Foucault's
History of Sexuality

Betty Friedan's
The Feminine Mystique

Saba Mahmood's
*The Politics of Piety:
The Islamic Revival and
the Feminist Subject*

Joan Wallach Scott's
*Gender and the
Politics of History*

Mary Wollstonecraft's
*A Vindication of the
Rights of Woman*

Virginia Woolf's
A Room of One's Own

Judith Butler's
Gender Trouble

Macat analyses are available from all good bookshops and libraries.

Access hundreds of analyses through one, multimedia tool.
Join free for one month **library.macat.com**

Macat Disciplines

*Access the greatest ideas and thinkers
across entire disciplines, including*

INEQUALITY

Ha-Joon Chang's, *Kicking Away the Ladder*

David Graeber's, *Debt: The First 5000 Years*

Robert E. Lucas's, *Why Doesn't Capital Flow from
Rich To Poor Countries?*

Thomas Piketty's, *Capital in the Twenty-First Century*

Amartya Sen's, *Inequality Re-Examined*

Mahbub Ul Haq's, *Reflections on Human Development*

Macat Disciplines

Access the greatest ideas and thinkers across entire disciplines, including

CRIMINOLOGY

Michelle Alexander's
The New Jim Crow: Mass Incarceration in the Age of Colorblindness

Michael R. Gottfredson & Travis Hirschi's
A General Theory of Crime

Elizabeth Loftus's
Eyewitness Testimony

Richard Herrnstein & Charles A. Murray's
The Bell Curve: Intelligence and Class Structure in American Life

Jay Macleod's
Ain't No Makin' It: Aspirations and Attainment in a Low-Income Neighborhood

Philip Zimbardo's
The Lucifer Effect

Macat Disciplines

Access the greatest ideas and thinkers across entire disciplines, including

Postcolonial Studies

Roland Barthes's *Mythologies*
Frantz Fanon's *Black Skin, White Masks*
Homi K. Bhabha's *The Location of Culture*
Gustavo Gutiérrez's *A Theology of Liberation*
Edward Said's *Orientalism*
Gayatri Chakravorty Spivak's *Can the Subaltern Speak?*

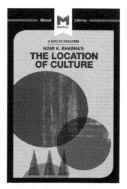

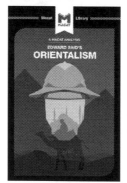

Macat Disciplines

Access the greatest ideas and thinkers across entire disciplines, including

GLOBALIZATION

Arjun Appadurai's, *Modernity at Large: Cultural Dimensions of Globalisation*

James Ferguson's, *The Anti-Politics Machine*

Geert Hofstede's, *Culture's Consequences*

Amartya Sen's, *Development as Freedom*

Macat analyses are available from all good bookshops and libraries.

Access hundreds of analyses through one, multimedia tool.
Join free for one month **library.macat.com**

Macat Pairs

*Analyse historical and modern issues
from opposite sides of an argument.
Pairs include:*

HOW TO RUN AN ECONOMY

John Maynard Keynes's
*The General Theory OF Employment,
Interest and Money*

Classical economics suggests that market economies
are self-correcting in times of recession or depression,
and tend toward full employment and output. But
English economist John Maynard Keynes disagrees.

In his ground-breaking 1936 study *The General
Theory*, Keynes argues that traditional economics
has misunderstood the causes of unemployment.
Employment is not determined by the price of labor;
it is directly linked to demand. Keynes believes market
economies are by nature unstable, and so require
government intervention. Spurred on by the social
catastrophe of the Great Depression of the 1930s,
he sets out to revolutionize the way the world thinks

Milton Friedman's
The Role of Monetary Policy

Friedman's 1968 paper changed the course of
economic theory. In just 17 pages, he demolished
existing theory and outlined an effective alternate
monetary policy designed to secure 'high employment,
stable prices and rapid growth.'

Friedman demonstrated that monetary policy plays
a vital role in broader economic stability and argued
that economists got their monetary policy wrong
in the 1950s and 1960s by misunderstanding the
relationship between inflation and unemployment.
Previous generations of economists had believed
that governments could permanently decrease
unemployment by permitting inflation—and vice versa.
Friedman's most original contribution was to show that
this supposed trade-off is an illusion that only works in
the short term.

Macat analyses are available from all good bookshops and libraries.

Access hundreds of analyses through one, multimedia tool.
Join free for one month **library.macat.com**

Macat Disciplines

Access the greatest ideas and thinkers across entire disciplines, including

THE FUTURE OF DEMOCRACY

Robert A. Dahl's, *Democracy and Its Critics*
Robert A. Dahl's, *Who Governs?*
Alexis De Toqueville's, *Democracy in America*
Niccolò Machiavelli's, *The Prince*
John Stuart Mill's, *On Liberty*
Robert D. Putnam's, *Bowling Alone*
Jean-Jacques Rousseau's, *The Social Contract*
Henry David Thoreau's, *Civil Disobedience*

Macat Disciplines

Access the greatest ideas and thinkers across entire disciplines, including

TOTALITARIANISM

Sheila Fitzpatrick's, *Everyday Stalinism*
Ian Kershaw's, *The "Hitler Myth"*
Timothy Snyder's, *Bloodlands*

Macat analyses are available from all good bookshops and libraries.

Access hundreds of analyses through one, multimedia tool.
Join free for one month **library.macat.com**

Macat Pairs

Analyse historical and modern issues from opposite sides of an argument. Pairs include:

RACE AND IDENTITY

Zora Neale Hurston's
Characteristics of Negro Expression

Using material collected on anthropological expeditions to the South, Zora Neale Hurston explains how expression in African American culture in the early twentieth century departs from the art of white America. At the time, African American art was often criticized for copying white culture. For Hurston, this criticism misunderstood how art works. European tradition views art as something fixed. But Hurston describes a creative process that is alive, ever-changing, and largely improvisational. She maintains that African American art works through a process called 'mimicry'—where an imitated object or verbal pattern, for example, is reshaped and altered until it becomes something new, novel—and worthy of attention.

Frantz Fanon's
Black Skin, White Masks

Black Skin, White Masks offers a radical analysis of the psychological effects of colonization on the colonized.

Fanon witnessed the effects of colonization first hand both in his birthplace, Martinique, and again later in life when he worked as a psychiatrist in another French colony, Algeria. His text is uncompromising in form and argument. He dissects the dehumanizing effects of colonialism, arguing that it destroys the native sense of identity, forcing people to adapt to an alien set of values—including a core belief that they are inferior. This results in deep psychological trauma.

Fanon's work played a pivotal role in the civil rights movements of the 1960s.

Macat Pairs

Analyse historical and modern issues from opposite sides of an argument. Pairs include:

INTERNATIONAL RELATIONS IN THE 21ST CENTURY

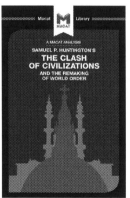

Samuel P. Huntington's
The Clash of Civilisations

In his highly influential 1996 book, Huntington offers a vision of a post-Cold War world in which conflict takes place not between competing ideologies but between cultures. The worst clash, he argues, will be between the Islamic world and the West: the West's arrogance and belief that its culture is a "gift" to the world will come into conflict with Islam's obstinacy and concern that its culture is under attack from a morally decadent "other."

Clash inspired much debate between different political schools of thought. But its greatest impact came in helping define American foreign policy in the wake of the 2001 terrorist attacks in New York and Washington.

Francis Fukuyama's
The End of History and the Last Man

Published in 1992, *The End of History and the Last Man* argues that capitalist democracy is the final destination for all societies. Fukuyama believed democracy triumphed during the Cold War because it lacks the "fundamental contradictions" inherent in communism and satisfies our yearning for freedom and equality. Democracy therefore marks the endpoint in the evolution of ideology, and so the "end of history." There will still be "events," but no fundamental change in ideology.

Macat Pairs

Analyse historical and modern issues from opposite sides of an argument. Pairs include:

ARE WE FUNDAMENTALLY GOOD - OR BAD?

Steven Pinker's
The Better Angels of Our Nature

Stephen Pinker's gloriously optimistic 2011 book argues that, despite humanity's biological tendency toward violence, we are, in fact, less violent today than ever before. To prove his case, Pinker lays out pages of detailed statistical evidence. For him, much of the credit for the decline goes to the eighteenth-century Enlightenment movement, whose ideas of liberty, tolerance, and respect for the value of human life filtered down through society and affected how people thought. That psychological change led to behavioral change—and overall we became more peaceful. Critics countered that humanity could never overcome the biological urge toward violence; others argued that Pinker's statistics were flawed.

Philip Zimbardo's
The Lucifer Effect

Some psychologists believe those who commit cruelty are innately evil. Zimbardo disagrees. In *The Lucifer Effect*, he argues that sometimes good people do evil things simply because of the situations they find themselves in, citing many historical examples to illustrate his point. Zimbardo details his 1971 Stanford prison experiment, where ordinary volunteers playing guards in a mock prison rapidly became abusive. But he also describes the tortures committed by US army personnel in Iraq's Abu Ghraib prison in 2003—and how he himself testified in defence of one of those guards. committed by US army personnel in Iraq's Abu Ghraib prison in 2003—and how he himself testified in defence of one of those guards.

Macat analyses are available from all good bookshops and libraries.

Access hundreds of analyses through one, multimedia tool.
Join free for one month **library.macat.com**

Macat Pairs

Analyse historical and modern issues from opposite sides of an argument. Pairs include:

HOW WE RELATE TO EACH OTHER AND SOCIETY

Jean-Jacques Rousseau's
The Social Contract

Rousseau's famous work sets out the radical concept of the 'social contract': a give-and-take relationship between individual freedom and social order.

If people are free to do as they like, governed only by their own sense of justice, they are also vulnerable to chaos and violence. To avoid this, Rousseau proposes, they should agree to give up some freedom to benefit from the protection of social and political organization. But this deal is only just if societies are led by the collective needs and desires of the people, and able to control the private interests of individuals. For Rousseau, the only legitimate form of government is rule by the people.

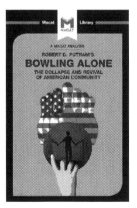

Robert D. Putnam's
Bowling Alone

In *Bowling Alone*, Robert Putnam argues that Americans have become disconnected from one another and from the institutions of their common life, and investigates the consequences of this change.

Looking at a range of indicators, from membership in formal organizations to the number of invitations being extended to informal dinner parties, Putnam demonstrates that Americans are interacting less and creating less "social capital" – with potentially disastrous implications for their society.

It would be difficult to overstate the impact of *Bowling Alone*, one of the most frequently cited social science publications of the last half-century.

Macat analyses are available from all good bookshops and libraries.

Access hundreds of analyses through one, multimedia tool.
Join free for one month **library.macat.com**

Printed in the United States
by Baker & Taylor Publisher Services